Ghosty Men

Ghosty Men

**The Strange but True Story of the Collyer Brothers,
New York's Greatest Hoarders**

An Urban Historical by

FRANZ LIDZ

BLOOMSBURY

Published by Bloomsbury, New York and London
Distributed to the trade by Holtzbrinck Publishers

Library of Congress Cataloging-in-Publication Data has been applied for.

ISBN 1–58234–311–X

First U.S. Edition 2003

1 3 5 7 9 10 8 6 4 2

Typeset by Hewer Text Ltd, Edinburgh
Printed in the United States of America
by R.R. Donnelley & Sons, Crawfordsville, Indiana

For those sardonic sisters, Gogo and Daisy Daisy

All art is the same – an attempt to fill an empty space.

– Samuel Beckett

Chapter 1

Homer Leaves Home

Homer Collyer left the moldering Harlem brownstone for the first time in seven years in a khaki canvas sack, lowered down a fire truck ladder like dirty laundry in a duffel bag.

Already famous as the "Hermits of Harlem," Homer, blind, paralyzed, and sixty-five, and his brother, Langley, sixty-one, had lived in the four-story mansion since 1909, gradually filling it with . . . *stuff*.

Harlem was fashionable, bourgeois, and white when the Collyers moved in, but they became reclusive in a neighborhood that became increasingly shabby, poor, and black.

Stray cats crying in the night were perhaps the first to sense that death had come to the house at Fifth Avenue and 128th Street.

For decades, Langley had fed a multitude of cats around midnight when he set out on his own nocturnal rounds, scavenging through the trash bins of the city. A wraithlike figure in ragged, Dickensian clothes, the old hoodoo rarely left the house during the daylight hours. He had created a sanctuary of junk for himself and his older brother. But on this morning – during the first dark hours of spring on March 21, 1947 – the cats remained hungry and unfed.

Dawn had already come when police received a call from a man who identified himself as "Charles Smith."

"There's a dead man at 2078 Fifth Avenue."

"Name of the deceased?" asked the cop on duty.

"Homer Collyer."

About ten o'clock, a police inspector and about fifteen patrolmen arrived at the decaying house. Reports of Homer's death had often brought police to the Collyer home over the years. But they had been inside only once.

Five years earlier, a police sergeant named John Collins, checking one more rumor that Homer had died, persuaded Langley to let him in through a basement door intricately wired shut against intruders. Collins stumbled along behind Langley for half an hour as he led the way through a pitch-black basement and upstairs through a booby-trapped labyrinth of rubbish.

He found Homer alive and indignant.

"I switched on my flashlight," he said. "And there was

2

Homer, sitting up like a mummy. He was on a cot, a burlap bag beneath him and an old overcoat on the foot of the cot.

"I am Homer L. Collyer, the lawyer," the old man said in a deep voice. "I want your name and shield number. I am not dead!"

"Why are you sitting with your knees up to your chin?" the sergeant asked.

"My legs are doubled by rheumatism. I can never lie down again."

So on this spring morning in 1947, new rumors of death brought a crowd of hundreds and then thousands to wait on the Harlem corner in a cold drizzle while police tried for two hours to get in. The cops closed off the street as it filled up with newspaper reporters, newsreel photographers, and cameramen from a new medium – television.

The house looked deserted. The doors were bolted and the ground-floor windows were covered with rusted iron grilles. The windows were all broken, shuttered, or stuffed with paper.

Police chopped a hole in the front door. Fumes foul with age and mildew billowed forth. The police peered into a solid wall of rotting junk amassed over the decades: shattered sawhorses and fractured frying pans, crushed umbrellas and rusted bicycles, broken baby carriages and smashed Christmas trees, chipped chandeliers and tattered toys, and everywhere, everywhere, newspapers – thousands and thousands of newspapers, stuffed under furniture, stacked in unsteady piles against walls, strewn in yellowing drifts across the floor.

At a quarter after twelve, the fire department ran a ladder up to a second-story window. Patrolman William Parker climbed up and into the still heart of the hoard. He flashed his light into a cavelike burrow.

"One DOA," he shouted down.

The dead man was Homer Collyer. He sat hunched on the floor about six feet from the window, his body emaciated, his knees pulled up to his chin. He wore only a tattered gray dressing gown. His cheeks were drawn; his dirty white hair and beard uncut for years hung in tangled locks to his waist. His right hand rested near a shriveled apple, a container of rancid milk, and a copy of the *Philadelphia Jewish Morning Journal* from Sunday, February 22, 1920.

"The place is like a maze," said Detective John Loughery, who followed Parker through the window. "We have to bend double to get through it all."

They dropped Homer to the sidewalk in the khaki body bag. A mortuary ambulance took him away. An autopsy showed that his stomach and digestive tract were empty. The medical examiner said he died of neglect.

At five o'clock the police boarded up the house.

"Where's Langley?" murmured the crowd. "Where's Langley?"

Chapter 2
The Lost Collyer Brother

My mother used to call my uncle Arthur the lost Collyer brother. I was never sure if by "lost" she meant missing, helpless, or that his real name was Langley.

I already knew who Langley was because my father told me cautionary tales about the Collyers as bedtime stories. He had a family full of Collyer brothers, and Uncle Arthur seemed to me much like Langley. Every time I went to visit I remembered the haunted house of the Collyers. Their story has stuck with me to this day, dragged along by my fear that Uncle Arthur would end up like Homer, lost in his junk.

My mom regarded her brother-in-law pretty much the way Tom Sawyer's aunt Polly regarded Huckleberry Finn. They both "cordially hated and dreaded" the irresistible attraction of vagabond outsiders who ignored order, convention, and even cleanliness.

Huck Finn scuffed through the dirt lanes of nineteenth-century St. Petersburg, Missouri, dressed in hand-me-down clothes "in perennial bloom and fluttering with rags." Uncle Arthur shuffles through the asphalt streets of twenty-first-century Brooklyn outfitted in layers of Salvation Army overcoats the color of bad weather.

While pirating with Huck on the Mississippi, Tom Sawyer's pockets harbored a lump of chalk, an India-rubber ball, three fishhooks, and "that kind of marbles known as 'sure 'nough crystal.'" While scavenging along the East River, Uncle Arthur's pockets often brim with his own schoolboy treasures: corks, bottle caps, and knots of used shoelaces.

Huck and Tom. Homer and Langley. The twains meet in Uncle Arthur, a small, lopsided, eternally boyish octogenarian with gentle brown eyes and ears like teacup handles. An urban prospector, he mines the neighborhoods taxi drivers ignore, trashmen neglect, and police suspect. And just as Tom admired Huck and delighted in his forbidden company, I am enchanted by Uncle Arthur.

Mostly, I admire his commitment to extreme squalor. Like the Collyers, Uncle Arthur has turned squalor into an art form. In my childhood memoir, *Unstrung Heroes*, I described spending the night of my eighth birthday at an apartment he then had in the Bronx. Towers of cereal cartons and soapboxes honeycombed the living room and spread into the kitchen.

Uncle Arthur's space was as enclosing, consoling, as Tom Sawyer's cave. Great jumbles of nubby pencils and chewed swizzle sticks crunched underfoot. Second-, third-, and seventh-hand books leaned against the windows as bulwarks against reality. Newspapers – thousands and thousands of newspapers – were everywhere: stuffed under furniture, stacked in unsteady piles against walls, strewn in yellowing drifts across the floor. Uncle Arthur's closets creaked with the overspill.

In Uncle Arthur's vault of shifting, sunlit dust, his papers close around you like a dark forest. Without him for a guide, you ran the risk of setting off one of his Collyerlike booby traps patched together from frayed rope, jam jars, telephone books. Still, at eight, I couldn't resist charging through the litter of letters and cards and coupons. Every misstep dislodged a big heap, setting off a sort of tidal wave across the apartment, dislodging other heaps in its progress.

Uncle Arthur started picking up stuff from the streets of the Lower East Side when he was only fifteen.

"In the days before the traffic lights went up in Manhattan I used to lead a blind man around Manhattan for ten dollars a week."

He speaks in a slow, deliberate way, as if he thinks before every word.

"People would give us money for shoelaces. He'd spend it on women. He'd go up to their apartments and I'd wait outside and get angry. I wanted to get something for my troubles. And I took shoelaces. That started me on my collection."

He was still only a nineteen-year-old novice collector when the Lidz family moved to a tiny tenement apartment in Harlem, only three blocks from the Collyer homestead. He already knew Homer and Langley were the preeminent junk collectors.

"I'd walk by their house and wonder what of value did they have. You gotta have brains to collect that much stuff," Uncle Arthur marvels. "I always wanted to get in touch with them. I always wanted to get in touch with anybody who collected as much as I did. They collected more. They had their junk up to the windows. I didn't have that much."

He envied the space the Collyers had in their twelve-room mansion. They eventually accumulated 180 tons of junk. But by the time he got to Brooklyn, Uncle Arthur was doing pretty well. Still, he never quite got over a feeling of not meeting the Collyers' high standards of junk connoisseurship.

"I save this, I save that," he says. "I mix it all together, the good and the bad. So it's my fault."

He particularly prized first-edition magazines, bus transfers, and parking tickets plucked from windshields.

"People just leave parking tickets on their cars," he says, wonderingly. "I must have found thousands of dollars' worth. Every day I could pick one up."

He regrets mixing his gems of junk with common everyday newspapers.

"I admit that's my mistake. I saved the papers because I used to like to read about politics."

Uncle Arthur finds his booty in back alleys, subway cars, train stations . . .

"Believe it or not I've never bought a single piece of junk. I found it all on the street. You'd be surprised what you find once you look. Pennies, nickels, dimes, safety pins, jacks, dice, mirrors, small bottles, dresser handles, screws, wire, cord, mothballs, cigarette packs, pens that say different things on them, bullets."

I remember him arriving at the doorstep of my boyhood home on Long Island, stoop-shouldered under the weight of the cast-off rubber balls and pickaxes and ironing boards he carried on his back like some slightly demented junk Sherpa from the Bronx. There has never been anyone quite like Uncle Arthur in my life, and there were times when it seemed that even one of him was too many. My mother didn't know what to make of my uncle, or what to *do* about him. That was what made him so fascinating.

Uncle Arthur is the last flowering of a generation of hoarders, an obsessive breed of Collyerian pack rats who never pass a Dumpster without lifting the lid. Hoarders are no longer tolerated in condominiums and cooperative apartments.

"My landlord doesn't like my hobby," concedes Uncle Arthur, "but I've got a lease."

He's not insensitive. He knows people sniff at his junk. Frequently.

"Collecting this junk," Uncle Arthur says, "they call me crazy, just because I got a lot of what no one else has.

"One out of ten people collect stuff. Most of the time people collect old things for the value of it. The difference between old things and old junk is that old things is what nobody has and old junk is what nobody wants."

Uncle Arthur spent a lifetime building an edifice of junk to withdraw into, but it was an edifice that was bound to topple. When I was eight I could hardly envision that it would be me who would level his fortress of ephemera.

Chapter 3
Helen and the Hermits

Helen Worden waited in a taxicab in front of the Collyer brothers' brownstone on a May night in 1938 when a rusty iron gate rasped open under a basement archway.

She described the sound as the sharp treble of a tuneless violin. She was a reporter on the old *World-Telegram* and she had come to unravel the mystery of the ghosty men who lived in the crumbling mansion.

She heard shuffling feet and the scrape of something being dragged across the sidewalk.

"What time is it?" she asked the cabdriver.

"Five minutes to midnight," he said.

She watched a wisp of a man in janitor's overalls separate himself from the shadows, pulling a large wooden box at the end of a rope.

"In the half-light," she said, "I was conscious of a white face and a drooping Victorian mustache."

She climbed out of the cab.

"Good evening, Langley Collyer," she said. "Your neighbor tells me you keep a rowboat in the attic and a Ford in the basement. Is that true?"

Langley hesitated at the curb, not at all taken aback.

"Yes and no," he said.

He was courteous and cultured and at ease, Worden recalled.

The boat and the car belonged to his father, a doctor at Bellevue, Langley said.

"Father used to carry it across to the Harlem River on his head, drop it in, and paddle down to the hospital every morning and back in the evening."

His father's Model T lay in bits in the basement.

"I never got around to putting it together after he died."

The saga of the Collyer brothers had begun with an exchange only slightly more askew than Stanley's greeting: "Dr. Livingstone, I presume."

Helen Worden broke the story that would fascinate New York for the next nine years. Two reclusive men who appeared in the sunlight about as often as Dracula became instant celebrities. The city's eight daily newspapers vied for scoops with each new turn in the story, like kids at an ice cream stand. "Harlem's Most Fascinating Mystery," the tabloids said.

Langley stood before her that first night in tattered clothes, a bicycle cap fifty years out of date pulled down over locks of gray hair that straggled out over his shoulders.

He rattled on like a man used to spending long hours in silence, and Worden was a good listener. He launched into a tirade against the neighborhood kids.

"These terrible children," he said. "They call me 'Spook.' They say I drag dead bodies into the house after dark and string them from our old elm tree."

He shook a fist at Harlem, Worden said.

"They break my windows. They make my life miserable. They even put a sign on my door saying THIS IS A GHOST HOUSE."

His father bought the house at 2078 Fifth Avenue for his mother when Harlem was a smart new neighborhood.

"We came to Harlem in 1909," Langley said. "It took ten vans to move our furniture."

His brother, Homer, a real estate lawyer, bought the house across the street at 2077 Fifth as an investment when the Triboro Bridge was built.

"My brother thought the neighborhood would pick up. Look at it now."

Worden listened. She'd spent her last half dozen years on the *World-Telegram* as a society reporter, listening to some of the more vain people in New York, the fading four hundred.

"Our family is one of the oldest in New York," he said. "The first Collyer came from England on the *Speedwell*, which was really better than the *Mayflower*."

He asserted the last vestige of a minute social snobbery as shabby as his clothes, meaningless to anybody except Bradfords, Brewsters, Winslows, and Collyers, and ignorant of the history of the *Speedwell*, a ship so leaky it never left England.

He rambled on. He never asked Worden what she was doing in Harlem at midnight.

"My great-grandfather, William Collyer, owned the largest shipyard on the East River waterfront. My mother and father were born at Tivoli on the Hudson. They were cousins of the Livingstons. Our people owned the first steamboats on the Hudson River."

The Livingstons were old family English patroons from the Hudson River Valley. Langley's mother, Susie, was a Livingston.

"Mother and Father were both great readers," he said. "In fact, Mother read Greek to us in the original. I have a smattering of that language myself."

He told Worden that his mother was an opera singer and that he had studied to be a concert pianist. He owned perhaps fourteen pianos, including one that Queen Victoria had given his mother.

"That piano's got a wonderful tone," he said. "I only play for pleasure now. I've long since given up public appearances."

"Why?" asked Worden.

"My last concert was at Carnegie Hall. Paderewski followed me. He got better notices than I. What was the use of going on?"

Worden then asked the wrong question: "Would you play for me?"

"Impossible!" he said. "I'd have to dust the house."

He tipped his cap, said good night, and scuttled off into the gloom, dragging the box after him, the box that contained the detritus from the New York night that eventually filled the house.

Worden was just making a switch from society reporting to writing news features. She'd started out on the *New York World* in 1926 after studying art in Paris. In 1931, she moved to the *World-Telegram*, where she wrote genre pieces like this excerpt of her report from aboard the SS *Queen Mary:* "Those who achieved a turn around the decks on the first night out include Lady Doverdale, Lord Jersey, Mrs. Robert A. Ramsdell, the Earl and Countess of Brandard . . ."

Dull stuff for a sharp reporter.

But she had already helped to drag society reporting toward modern times. A reviewer praising her book *Society Circus* said she'd come a long way from "the sedate chronicle of floral decoration and frocks.

"She gleans her most illuminating data from the gossip revelations of trades-people, caterers, dressmakers and head-waiters."

She'd gone out to Harlem in May 1938 on a story about a woman acquitted of murder. In *Out of This World*, her book about the Collyers and other hermits, she recalls chatting with the woman's father, an old German music master.

"When I bought this house," he said, "Harlem was a wonderful neighborhood."

He lived on 128th Street, just a few doors down from the Collyers.

"The millionaires of the city used to pace their trotters up and down Lenox Avenue. There was fine music at Pabst's 125th Street. Ladies went calling in Victorias."

Worden said she was still in a nostalgic mood when she

walked over to Fifth Avenue and the dilapidated mansion caught her attention.

"Though apparently deserted," she said, "the house bore neither a for-rent nor a for-sale sign. That intrigued me."

An African-American woman sunning herself on a nearby stoop offered the neighborhood myth.

"Oh, that's where Langley Collyer lives," she said. "His ma and pa and brother are supposed to be lying dead in there. Leastwise nobody's seen them in years. Langley's mighty rich." The woman patted the stoop. "He owns this house, too. Folks 'round here call him the ghosty man."

The ghosty man?

"Yes, ma'am. He only comes out after dark."

Worden was at the Collyers' doorstep less than twenty-four hours later. And she would cover the story with dogged tenacity for most of the next decade.

She made the Collyers famous. They're recalled even today when an elderly recluse dies amid an accumulation of stuff. And more than a half century later, New York City firefighters still refer to an emergency call to a junk-jammed home as a "Collyer."

Worden even became something of an aficionado of hermits. She chronicled the lives of a dozen and a half in *Out of This World.*

"We all have something of the hermit in us," she said.

She's all but forgotten today. She was a top woman reporter in New York for more than thirty years. Eleanor Roosevelt presented her with the New York Newspaper Women's Club Award for best feature writing in 1941. But now she doesn't even turn up in feminist collections of journalism.

Even Langley would berate her.

Consolidated Edison servicemen arrived one night in 1939 to take out the company's meters. After all, the Collyers hadn't used gas or electricity since 1928. "We paid our bills promptly," Langley said, "but they cut off our service claiming it was 'dangerous to continue.'"

He told a reporter Con Ed ignored his demands to restore service. He contended that a public utility refusing to supply service to an individual is subject to a fine of ten dollars a day. He figured Con Ed owed him for 3,650 days he'd been without gas, thirty-six thousand, five hundred dollars.

For a while, Langley tried to make his own electricity with an automobile generator. He and his brother lit the house with acetylene lamps. Langley said the telephone was disconnected in 1917 after they were billed for "long-distance calls we didn't make."

They quit using water and steam heat about the same time. Nobody quite knows what they did about personal hygiene, if anything. They cooked and lit the house with kerosene, but lived much of the time in the dark.

"Homer can't see, so he doesn't need light," Langley explained. "As for me, I prefer it a trifle shady."

In April 1939, Con Ed workmen, police, reporters, photographers, and a bemused crowd of neighbors besieged the Collyers in the house. The brothers kept quiet until cops and a meter reader pushed in a basement door. A barricade of rubble blocked them.

Langley appeared at an upper window.

"You've no right to break in my house," he screamed.

"The boys just want the meters," a police sergeant replied.

Langley withdrew and half an hour later appeared in an areaway. A gasman snatched a meter off the wall, and when Langley tried to snatch it back, someone hit him in the stomach with a stick.

"Take your meters!" he said, with the hauteur of a man who claimed ancestors among the Pilgrims.

Then he spotted Worden.

"He turned to me, shaking his fist: 'You're to blame for this.'"

And, of course, she was.

Chapter 4
Homer's Odyssey

Homer Collyer spent most of the last years of his life with his eyes closed. He had lost his sight in the fall of 1934.

So he and Langley had come up with their own home treatment. He would rest his eyes and eat one hundred oranges a week.

"You must remember we are the sons of a doctor," Langley said. "We have a medical library of fifteen thousand books in the house. Homer and I decided we would not call in any doctor. You see, we knew too much about medicine.

"Doctors would remove Homer's optic nerve and he would be blind forever. No, we decided to do it our own way – by diet and rest."

In 1946, after perhaps 67,600 oranges, he said, "Homer's vision is improving."

The brothers were both intelligent and a little too well educated for their father, Dr. Herman Collyer, a gynecologist at Bellevue, where Homer would end up for an autopsy in 1947.

"Too much education is bad," the doctor said. "My boys know too much."

Langley graduated with an engineering degree from Columbia, and Homer studied law at City College of New York and went on to earn advanced degrees in law at Columbia, where he graduated Phi Beta Kappa, class of 1904.

Herman and his wife, Susie, were first cousins.

"Quite society," said cousin Charles Collyer. "Always did the right thing."

Well, maybe not always.

Susie came from a seafaring riverboat family whose men seemed to drift around the world in search of pretty woman. One found his in Brazil, another in Japan. Proper relatives sniffed at offspring exotically named Carlotta and Morocco. But in those Victorian days women who led unconventional lives were often completely ostracized.

And Susie was certainly not conventional. She was a strong-willed, black-eyed, black-haired beauty with a fine singing voice. She sang operatic roles at the Academy of Music on Fourteenth Street, the grand opera house of the last half of the nineteenth century.

She soon fell in love with the young intern Herman, and they moved into a cold-water flat at Thirty-fifth Street and Third Avenue. Both Homer and Langley were born there.

Helen Worden thought Susie dominated the family. Psycho-analysts at the time suggested Susie's boys were Oedipal wrecks who could hardly peek out from beneath her Freudian slip. She gave Langley his first piano lesson and pushed Homer to excel at Columbia. When Herman wanted to turn the Harlem house into a sanitarium, she said no. In 1918 he moved out to a house on West Seventy-seventh Street, where he lived until his death in 1923.

The brothers lived on with their mother until she died six years later. Langley played a few recitals and took Mother to the opera. But only Homer ever held a real job.

In 1928 and 1929, he worked as an admiralty lawyer for John McMullen, a Wall Street attorney who was more or less the family lawyer.

"Homer delighted in having people take him for a poor eccentric man," McMullen told the *New York Sun*. "Then he would prove he was otherwise by pulling out a roll of bills and going into a discussion that showed he was not eccentric."

Maybe not eccentric, but certainly quirky. Among other things he habitually wore clothes fashionable about 1910.

"His poor attire aroused suspicions," McMullen recalled.

He ran into trouble in Stamford, Connecticut, where he was dispatched to deliver a deed to a certain John Cabot.

Homer looked like a suspicious character to clerks at the bank where he asked directions. They sent him to the police station next door. The police followed him to the Cabot mansion, where the butler made him wait outside until the master returned.

"Mr. Cabot came home and he and Homer went inside," McMullen said. "They found they had something in common – both were graduates of Columbia. Homer was invited to dinner. The butler was flabbergasted. That pleased Homer no end."

So Collyer sat down with Cabot, and no doubt they compared class rings before launching into robust choruses of "Roar, Lion, Roar."

Homer took charge when his mother died in 1929. No one knows quite why, but with the help of an undertaker he spirited her body out of the house through a parlor window in the middle of the night. They drove her out to Cypress Hills Cemetery in Brooklyn, where they buried her next to Herman in the Collyer family plot.

Homer brought a strong streak of Bartleby the Scrivener to

his next job, for a title insurance company, in 1930. He even looked liked the Herman Melville Wall Street law-copyist who addressed life with the words "I would prefer not to."

"He was as musty in appearance as one of his books," said Saul Fromkes, head of the City Title Insurance Company, at 32 Broadway.

He recalled Homer as a cultured gentleman who wore his hair long, his sideburns thick, and his collars high. He always carried a small roll of newspapers and, like Bartleby, copied his abstracts in a fine, literate hand.

"He came to us without any recommendations," Fromkes told Worden when she wrote for the *World-Telegram*. "Just wandered into our office and said he wanted work. After talking to him five minutes I saw he thoroughly understood the legal aspects of title research."

Homer was as fiercely protective of his private life as Bartleby was. He worked for City Title two years before Fromkes realized he walked the eight miles from Harlem every day. Homer would never spring for the five-cent subway ride. He thought it was a waste of money.

"Yet he always gave the impression he had plenty," Fromkes said. "That is until I picked up his roll of newspapers and found a lunch wrapped in it. Another time when I was arguing Greek philosophy with him, I happened to glance at his shoes." The soles were paper thin, and had worn through in spots. Fromkes offered him a retroactive raise on the spot.

Homer turned around and walked home and never came back. He never even picked up his last check.

About that time he and Langley showed up at the office of a real estate agent named Claremont Morris, who sold them the house across the street, at 2077 Fifth Avenue.

"Homer did the talking," Morris told Worden. "He thought 2077 a good investment."

Homer believed the Triboro Bridge, just then being built, would revive real estate values in Harlem. He thought he might break the building up into rental apartments. He never did.

"I let him have it for exactly what I paid for it," said Morris, who evidently didn't think Harlem was on the verge of a boom.

"They met me at the Farmers Loan and Trust Company in old-fashioned clothes, gates-ajar collars, high old-time socks and queer old hats."

The brothers pulled the money out of their pockets – seventy-five hundred dollars in cash.

Morris became the only person the Collyers ever welcomed inside their house. He said it was like an Egyptian tomb.

"The windows, what was left of them, hadn't been washed in years," he recounted for Worden. "Those broken by neighborhood boys had been replaced by boards. Great piles of newspapers, boxes and old wood were heaped in the hall. Beyond the scattered sections of the automobile stood a couple of pianos. Langley told me he had more, ten, I believe. Even in daylight it was so dark Langley held a lamp to guide me."

Langley told him they had simplified their lives by using neither gas nor electricity. They had simplified their diet, too.

"I believe they lived for the most part on peanut butter and black bread," Morris said.

The Collyers astonished him by later paying a "courtesy call" to his Gramercy Park home one night at ten o'clock. They stayed until two A.M. talking art, music, and literature.

"Langley was very musical," Morris said. "He played extremely well."

A bit of Chopin, it seems. Then he tuned the piano.

"Very creditably," Morris said.

He insisted on seeing them home at the end of the evening.

"I didn't realize they intended to walk from Gramercy Park to Harlem."

That's a bracing stroll of about one hundred blocks.

"I gave out at Eighty-sixth Street," he said.

He persuaded them to take the Third Avenue el the rest of the way.

"That was the last time they came to call. I heard later that someone had attempted to break into their house. After that the two never left it at the same time."

He saw Homer once more, about ten o'clock on a winter's evening in 1934. He roused Homer by tapping on a drainpipe.

"I walked around the block with him," Morris said. "He told me he was going blind and would never come out again. He seemed quite philosophical about it. He said there was no use to go out if you couldn't see and no need to go to your office if you couldn't read."

As in most of the Collyer brothers' peculiarities, there was a perfectly skewed logic.

After that no one seems to have seen Homer outside the house except for a fleeting moment early on New Year's Day 1940. Like figures from a Beckett play, they were seen lugging a tree across Fifth Avenue, Langley leading the blind Homer.

Homer retired to his pallet and the long, timeless darkness of the blind. Struck by rheumatism in 1940, he sat for seven years with his legs doubled up to his chin to ease the pain of paralysis.

His life became a long dialogue with Langley.

"I used to read to him," Langley told the *New York Herald Tribune* in 1942. "We had all the classics in our library. I used to read Shakespeare and Dickens, but my eyes went bad, and I stopped. So now we just talk and listen to the radio."

Langley, whose degree from Columbia was in engineering, hooked up an old crystal set to a storage battery.

"When Homer first lost his sight he used to see visions of beautiful buildings – always in red. He would describe them to me, and I would try to paint them just as he directed. I got some very interesting results. Someday, when Homer regains his sight, I will show the paintings to him."

Homer sat with his eyes closed against his blindness, awaiting his cure from his diet of oranges. "He really never sleeps," Langley said. "I have to care for him day and night. I cook his meals and have to cut up his meat into little cubes so he can eat it with a spoon. I have to bathe him and tend to all his wants."

Langley had become his brother's keeper.

Chapter 5
Such Stuff As Dreams Are Made On

The wooden cars of the Cyclone roller coaster lurched slowly heavenward, inch by ominous inch, before reaching the ride's first precipice and falling eighty-five stomach-shuddering feet. The Cyclone stood as a white-knuckle monument to grander days when Coney Island, the slender, sandy bar that shelters Brooklyn from the Atlantic Ocean, was called Sodom by the Sea.

It was summer in the late 1950s, and three of the five Lidz brothers were at Coney. The other two were in insane asylums. I was in the first car with my father's only mildly unbalanced oldest brother, Danny, who whooped and hollered, his tongue flopping out like a red leather bookmark.

Two rows back sat my father and my kid sister, Sandy. I figured Uncle Arthur was somewhere behind them, but when the ride was over, I looked back and didn't see him. I wondered if he'd fallen out.

At the exit stood my mother, whose dislike for roller coaster rides and my uncles was about equal. That day she was especially annoyed. Uncle Arthur had refused to spend the twenty-five cents for the subway from the Bronx – "It's too expensive" – and would join us only if we picked up him and Uncle Danny on our way from Long Island. "Why don't we mail him a quarter?" my mother asked my father. After much more griping from my mother, we detoured to the Bronx.

When I got off the Cyclone, I asked her, "Where's Uncle Arthur?"

"Where do you think?" she said with that weary, seen-it-all expression common to mothers at amusement parks.

"Buying a hot dog?"

She pointed. "Look over there."

"Over there" was beneath the tracks, where Uncle Arthur was hunched over, scavenging for additions to his collections.

He was quite a sight in the hot July sun. He wore a tweed overcoat over a green-and-white-striped summertime blazer and layers and layers of winter clothes, corduroy trousers rolled to lawyer's length, and several multicolored flannel shirts. The stubble on his chin made him look like he'd been on a stakeout for three days.

I scampered over and asked: "Whatcha got?"

He reached inside one of the shopping bags he had brought along and drew forth keys, coins, gum, a smashed camera, a hearing aid.

"Anything for me?" asked Sandy.

Uncle Arthur offered a set of dentures. Sandy grimaced, backed away, and hid behind my mother. She thought he was more alarming than charming.

"I'll take 'em," I said. I could always find a use for false teeth.

"Give it back to your uncle," said my mother sharply. "It's trash."

"Junk," Arthur, the connoisseur, said proudly.

"Whoever found anything valuable under a roller coaster?"

"Emilio Franco," said my father, the pedant, beginning his lecture on the mute West Virginia coal miner who found his voice on the Cyclone. Emilio screamed on the second descent, my father said, and spoke his first words in six years as he disembarked.

"What were they?" I asked.

" 'I feel sick,' " my father said.

My father discussed John McSorley, the proprietor of the venerated East Seventh Street alehouse, who collected wishbones from holiday turkeys and strung them over the bar, where they gathered dust for generations.

"The man who collected distances was very unusual," my father said swiftly. He packed more words into a minute than Uncle Arthur could in an hour.

"He wore a pedometer everywhere he went and recorded the times and distances of his walks from his apartment. He lived five miles and sixty-four minutes from Wall Street."

As Uncle Arthur might, the distance collector had recorded the number of socks he wore out en route to the New York World's Fair, the Cloisters, and the Tree of Hope in Harlem.

Uncle Arthur himself collected used socks, other people's socks. I wondered if he had any of Pedometer Man's.

Uncle Arthur was a lot like Langley Collyer. But he never played an instrument and he made his daily rounds in the daylight. He and Uncle Danny roomed together in the Bronx. Like the Collyers, they had lived with their mother until her death. That was fifty years for Danny and thirty-eight for Arthur. They sat by her bedside holding her hands when she died in 1953. But they didn't spirit her out the window. They sat *shivah* like good Jewish boys.

Both were walking messengers, which gave Uncle Arthur access to junk in all five boroughs. He brought his daily pickings back to the Bronx apartment, much to Uncle Danny's chagrin. A paranoid of unparalleled persistence, Danny pulled down the shades and nailed them to the wall so that prying eyes could never see the junk.

Uncle Arthur's junk mania may have begun at the end of World War I when he was only three years old. In 1918 his thirteen-year-old brother, Leo, had the job of removing every third bulb from the strings along the beach at Coney Island. Somehow that was supposed to confuse German zeppelins that might attack New York. He brought spent bulbs home to little Arthur, who was fascinated by their smooth, shiny roundness. They broke one by one as he grew older. But he still had a few even as an adult.

When he was old enough, Arthur would take the F train to the beach at Coney Island for swims with his brothers. He'd browse through the trash cans on the boardwalk for collectible junk. Coney Island was still aglow with Steeplechase Park and Luna Park and the lights along the boardwalk, and hot dogs at Nathan's cost five cents. New Yorkers came out on the BMT for a modest vacation in this "Empire of the Nickel." They stayed in tiny apartments and flimsy screened bungalows in summer colonies that were mostly white and Jewish.

When we rode the Cyclone, Coney Island was as frowsy as Arthur and a little scary to a grade-school kid. Luna Park was gone, cleared out for upscale housing. Steeplechase Park was on its last legs. It closed in 1965, after sixty-eight thrilling years, leaving the Parachute Jump as the derelict Eiffel Tower of Brooklyn. Nathan's – heaven forfend! – was selling frogs' legs.

Jews were starting to summer elsewhere, and the cottages were filling up with poor black families displaced by so-called urban renewal. Uncle Arthur fit right into the untidy decrepitude of Surf Avenue. The rest of my suburban Long Island family – even Uncle Danny, in his aggressively puce Arrow shirt – seemed to have beamed down from a distant galaxy.

By the time my father concluded his dissertation on whimsical collectors, my mother was fed up with Coney Island.

"Let's go to a museum," she said.

"Let's go to the circus," my sister whined.

"I know a place that's both," said Uncle Arthur.

"What's that, Arthur?" asked my mother.

"Hubert's," he said. "It's a museum and it's a flea circus."

"Well, if there's anybody who should know about fleas, Arthur, it's you."

Uncle Arthur nodded. He didn't get the joke.

"Arthur and fleas have *one* thing in common," cracked my father.

"What's that?" I asked.

"An aversion to vacuum cleaners."

Uncle Arthur nodded again. He didn't get that one, either. He *did* collect vacuum cleaners. Quite proudly, in fact.

"I'm not going to a flea circus, not me," Sandy said.

"*I* am," I said.

We all piled into our Nash Rambler and motored to Manhattan. Much to my mother's chagrin, Uncle Danny, the paranoid, made my father detour before the Gowanus Expressway, just in case we were being tailed.

My mother, dismissively: "By whom?"

Uncle Danny, accusingly: "You tell *me*, Selma."

Even while sitting still in the Nash, there was a sort of turbulence about Uncle Danny, a constant, restless, unfocused energy, like a candy wrapper fluttering in the breeze.

We dropped off my mom and Sandy at the Metropolitan Museum of Art. Uncle Danny, Uncle Arthur, my father, and I went to Hubert's Museum and Flea Circus.

Hubert's had been on Forty-second Street near Eighth Avenue for about forty years when we arrived. The museum would last only until 1965, when it became a peep-show palace. In five more years the top three floors would become a gay brothel called the Barracks.

The building started out in 1872 as a Roman Catholic

school for what the 1894 *King's Handbook of New York City* called "boys of refined families." Around the turn of the century, the great architectural firm of McKim, Mead & White converted the school into "a bachelor apartment house" called The Percival.

In 1908, Forty-second Street was smack in the heart of the city's burgeoning theater district, and The Percival became John L. Murray's Roman Gardens, an exotic restaurant with latticework pergolas, two marble mosaic fountains designed by Stanford White for the 1893 Chicago World's Fair, and a blue ceiling with electric stars.

The Roman Gardens succumbed to Prohibition, and Hubert's moved into the building, heralding another transformation of Forty-second Street, this time into a sideshow atmosphere that hardened into a porn strip.

When we got to Hubert's in the fifties, the first floor boasted a splendid collection of dubious curiosa. A quarter got you in to see display cases of jarred specimens. Among the assorted pathological and anatomical anomalies were a two-headed piglet and a puppy with six legs.

"This dog required two fire hydrants," declaimed a barker in a derby hat and brass-buttoned vest.

"What a pisser!" said my father.

Well, *I* laughed.

Uncle Arthur's small expressive face seemed to set into an almost spellbound concentration. He was studying posters of Velma the Headless Woman, Susi the Elephant Girl, and The Amazing Lintini, whose powers of amazement apparently derived from his four feet and sixteen toes.

"How many socks does he wear?" Uncle Arthur asked. Collecting was never far from his mind.

I marveled at the two-headed baby preserved in an immense jar of formaldehyde and guaranteed not to be Siamese twins, the giant killer rat of Cambodia that could gnaw a man's arm off in thirty seconds, and the guy who stuffed white mice into his mouth for no reason I could understand.

"He eats golf balls, too," Uncle Arthur said. I couldn't understand that either. I knew the guy didn't really swallow the mice, and I hoped he didn't swallow golf balls.

But I could understand why Uncle Arthur loved this place.

"It's got the best junk in the world," he said dreamily.

As Uncle Arthur jammed two dozen of Hubert's pamphlets into the inner pocket of his outer coat, the barker rattled off his spiel for the main event:

"Ladies and gentlemen, once every hour, Hubert's Museum is proud to present Professor Heckler's Traveling Flea Circus.

In the enclosure you are going to see dozens of real live trained performing fleas – fleas that juggle, jump through hoops, play football, operate a miniature merry-go-round, and are hitched to a tiny chariot to run an actual race."

Another quarter (my father was paying) got us into the basement flea circus. We walked down a flight of steps and through a curtain to the edge of a big round white table with a bright light overhead and a thick magnifying glass all the way around. One ring is all a flea circus needs.

In the middle was miniature circus equipment: the chariots, a high wire, a diving platform with a tiny bucket, a step ladder, a tricycle, and a toy cannon. The flea master, Professor Heckler, stood across from me with an array of little mother-of-pearl boxes. He reached into one with a pair of tweezers and plucked out a black speck. "My performers are invisible to the naked eye," said the professor. Not *my* naked eye – I reckoned the flea was about as big as a freckle.

Rumpled and lumbering, with a line of patter as weary as his smile, the professor introduced "Paddy the Irish flea." Paddy stepped out smartly, waving an itsy-bitsy Irish flag. You really had to squint through the magnifying glass to see him.

My father, the skeptic, asked: "How do you know he's Irish?"

"By his accent," snapped the maestro.

He explained that there were 131 kinds of fleas. But the human fleas called *Pulex irritans* were the best: "The human flea excels all others in endurance, length of life, and intelligence."

Dog fleas, he said, died by the time you got them trained.

"A pity," said my father, always sensitive to the plight of insects.

Uncle Arthur asked, "How do you know they're smart?"

"I put new fleas in a closed jar," the flea master said. "They jump up and hit their head against the lid. Intelligent fleas stop jumping."

"How do you know they're not just tired?" Uncle Arthur said.

The flea master ignored Uncle Arthur. He said the smart fleas got little gold collars and went to flea school. The dumb ones he released into the world to fend for themselves.

"It's tough being a flea," Uncle Danny said, genuinely sympathetic.

Paddy returned to his mother-of-pearl quarters, and his place was taken by a flea who ran with a tiny football through tiny goalposts.

"Please cheer," said the flea master.

I did.

"Louder, please. Fleas have very small ears."

The next flea pulled the cannon by a thread attached to its collar. Another lay on its back twirling a ball. A third climbed to the diving platform, and from that great flea height dove into the bucket, splashing droplets on the table.

Uncle Arthur jumped back as if he were about to be drenched.

"The *Pulex irritans* is a world-champion jumper," intoned Professor Heckler. "If it were the size of a man, it could leap over the Great Pyramid of Giza in a single bound."

"What's the point?" asked Uncle Arthur.

Professor Heckler brushed off the remark like he would one of his peskier pupils. "Fleas can pull one hundred twenty thousand times their weight," he said. "A Mandarin emperor in the Liao Dynasty hunted them with a tiny crossbow."

Uncle Danny and I bobbed our heads in unison. Now, *that* was impressive.

Fleas leaped through flaming hoops, like lions under the big top. Hurdlers dashed the flea equivalent of one hundred yards, maybe a foot. Two-flea teams raced chariots with vest-button wheels around the table as if they were centurions in the Colosseum. The winner galloped through the front door of a train-set building marked MOTEL. "It's a fleabag," the professor explained.

We watched raptly; even my father was captivated.

The tightwire flea strutted back and forth across a black silk thread all of five inches above the table. It balanced a one-and-a-half-inch pole on one side and a tiny chair on the other.

"Don't fall. Don't fall off," Uncle Arthur said, transfixed and concerned.

I marveled, too, but as an eight-year-old sophisticate I knew a five-inch fall wouldn't be fatal even for a flea. An ant . . . maybe.

After the show was over I asked, "What do they eat?"

The flea master rolled up his sleeve and showed us an arm pimpled with red welts.

"I feed them. Two times a day, three when we have a matinee."

"Does anyone want to try?" he asked.

I volunteered Uncle Arthur.

The flea master opened one of his mother-of-pearl boxes. He flecked an invisible flea onto Arthur's wrist with a magician's sleight-of-hand move. I never thought there really was a flea. But Uncle Arthur did.

He began frantically pulling off his clothes, layer by layer, like a Minsky stripper. He got thinner and thinner until he stood there in his undershirt, gaunt and scrawny and, I thought, as weightless as a flea.

Chapter 6
Harlem Degentrified

Homer and Langley Collyer were already young men when their father moved the family to a handsome, newly built brownstone Harlem town house in 1909. Homer had his law degree from Columbia and Langley was just finishing his studies there. They taught Sunday School at Trinity Church in Wall Street. They seemed normal enough. But though waves of transformation swept over Harlem, they would never again live anywhere else. They stayed while the house crumbled around them. They turned into reclusive hermits who barely acknowledged the passing of time. They remained locked in a turn-of-the-century time warp through both world wars, the Great Depression, and the devolution of Harlem from an exclusive white suburb to a poor black ghetto.

Herman Collyer may have thought he was buying into a real estate boom sparked by the coming of the Lenox Avenue line, but he just caught the bust.

In his classic *Harlem: The Making of a Ghetto*, Gilbert Osofsky says, "People generally took it for granted that Harlem would develop into an exclusive, stable, upper- and upper-middle-class community: 'a neighborhood very genteel.'"

And, it went without saying, totally white.

Newly affluent immigrants from the Lower East Side surged into Harlem at the end of the nineteenth century. New York City annexed Harlem in 1873, when it was an odd combination of a country retreat for the rich and shantytowns where squatters raised produce and livestock for the local markets. So many hogs wandered along 125th Street, it was known as Pig Alley.

The city filled 1,350 acres of marshland in 1870 and opened the wide boulevards north of Central Park. Real estate speculators, including Tweed Ring ward heelers, built more and more blocks of homes and apartments, then sold and resold them over and over again until the boom busted.

Most of the older buildings in Harlem today were built during this era. The new Harlemites who filled them formed the Harlem Yacht Club, the Harlem Literary Society, the Harlem Philharmonic Orchestra, the Harlem Democratic and Republican Clubs, the Harlem branches of the Daughters of the American Revolution and Loyal Women of American Liberty. All white.

125th Street was already the main drag. When Dr. Collyer moved his family onto Fifth Avenue at 128th Street, Fanny Brice and Sophie Tucker played Hurtig and Seamon's Music Hall – which became the Apollo on January 26, 1934. Oscar Hammerstein I built fifty town houses early in the boom, when Harlem was still a country shantytown, and then opened his Harlem Opera House on 125th Street in 1889 to draw people north. Edwin Booth, Lillian Russell, Otis Skinner, and John Drew Barrymore performed there. Hammerstein quickly opened his second theater, the Columbia, down the street, where George M. Cohan and Walter Damrosch were headliners. The fashionable rich dined at Pabst's Harlem Restaurant, the biggest in New York City, when it served its first sauerbraten and dumplings in 1900. Twenty years later it was a Kress five-and-ten.

Swells drove all manner of carriages along the Harlem River Speedway, a road that opened in 1898 especially designed for the high-stepping trotters of gold-plated sportsmen. Harlem River Drive follows the same route today.

A decade after he opened the Waldorf Hotel at Fifth Avenue and Thirty-fourth Street – the future site of the Empire State

Building – William Waldorf Astor built the block-long Graham Court at Seventh Avenue and 116th Street for those same swells. Astor bragged about the cost, five hundred thousand dollars, a hefty sum in those days. No African-American was allowed to live there until 1928. Graham Court survives, rejuvenated as one of the more chic addresses in Harlem for smart young people, black and white.

In 1891, Stanford White, the architect of Madison Square Garden, the Washington Arch, and Grand Central Terminal, was commissioned to design 106 buildings on land owned by the Equitable Life Assurance Society along 138th and 139th streets. They were luxurious brownstones with ten to sixteen rooms set back twelve feet from the street, with driveways ornamented by flowerbeds.

Only the prosperous could afford them – but they weren't buying.

Speculation in Harlem real estate had spread all over Manhattan, even to the coffeehouses of Little Italy and the tearooms of the Lower East Side. When Harlem's hot property heyday peaked about 1900, speculators were gambling that the coming of the elevated subway, that splendid oxymoron, would bring more and more people and keep the boom going. But they didn't come fast enough to fill the empty apartment blocks. The boosterism that had moved the *Harlem Local Reporter* to chirp in 1890 of "the greatness that lies in store for Harlem" was dead by 1904.

The vast, sprawling jumble that is black Harlem began in 1903 when Philip A. Payton, Jr., "the Father of Colored Harlem," moved African-American families into an apartment house at 31 West 134th Street.

In the early nineteenth century, Manhattan's small free black population lived on the edge of the city in the neighborhood called "Negro Plantations" at the notorious Five Points slum, where City Hall now stands. After the end of slavery in New York in 1827, blacks drifted north to enclaves like "Little Africa" in Greenwich Village. But at the end of the Civil War there were only 9,943 blacks in New York, fewer than in 1820. Only forty-four owned enough property to vote.

After his American visit in 1842, Charles Dickens wrote that blacks lived in places "dogs would howl to lie, [where] men and women slink off to sleep, forcing the dislodged rats to move away . . ."

New York's African-American population began to increase only after the end of Reconstruction in the South and with the rise of immigration from the West Indies. Blacks settled in such raffishly named West Side outposts as Hell's Kitchen (West

Thirtieth Street to West Fifty-ninth, from Seventh Avenue to the Hudson River), San Juan Hill (north of Columbus Circle), the Tenderloin (from the West Twenties to the West Sixties near Sixth, Seventh and Eighth avenues), and its cultural subdivision, Negro Bohemia.

Echoing Dickens at the turn of the twentieth century, *Harper's Weekly* wrote with classic condescension of the Tenderloin: "Amid scenes of indescribable squalor and tawdry finery dwell the Negroes, leading their light-hearted lives of pleasure, confusion, music, noise and fierce fights."

African-Americans had already become targets of recurring racist violence. In the bloody convulsion of Manhattan's 1863 Draft Riots, immigrants opposed to Union conscription upended the city and lynched blacks. White mobs, unobstructed if not encouraged by police, ravaged Hell's Kitchen in 1900, and San Juan Hill five years later. Harlem landlords – including newly formed black real estate companies led by Philip Payton – offered sanctuary in buildings left empty by the boom's collapse, with a premium "Negro" surcharge added to their rent. By the end of the 1920s, blacks in Harlem paid up to 40 percent more than the average white New Yorker.

World War I lured more Southern blacks north in search of higher wages, and by the end of the war the African-American population was 152,000. The ingathering that began during World War I quickened through the twenties. Southern blacks streamed north in what has become known as the Great Migration. Harlem was always the prized destination. West Indians came, from Jamaica and Barbados and the Bahamas. New York attracted ten times more foreign-born blacks than any other American city.

White residents fought to block the influx.

A letter to *The New York Times* asked, "Can they do nothing to put a restriction on the invasion of the Negro into Harlem . . . ? They're coming closer all the time."

And a Lenox Avenue realty company received a letter more threatening: "We have been informed of your intention to rent your house at 46 West 117th Street to Negro tenants. This is wholly un-American, and is totally against our principles. We ask you in a gentlemanly way to rescind your order, or unpleasant things may happen. May your decision be the right one." The letter was signed "K.K.K. Realm 7, Chapter 3."

Restrictive covenants did ban selling or renting to blacks. But they collapsed as more whites – 119,000 between 1920 and 1930 – left Harlem and its burgeoning black population for Queens, Brooklyn, and the Bronx.

In 1919, for instance, after restricting sales to whites for two decades, Equitable Life grudgingly sold White's lovely brownstones to African-Americans. Without the slightest sense of irony they were advertised as "the finest group of Negro residences in the country." They were snapped up in eight months by well-to-do blacks like Eubie Blake, ragtime piano player and songwriter; Fletcher Henderson, bandleader; Will Marion Cook, composer; and Harry Wills, the heavyweight boxer Jack Dempsey ducked. And 138th and 139th streets became "Striver's Row," and the old houses remain very desirable residences for today's strivers.

The Harlem Renaissance blossomed in the middle 1920s with new young writers like Countee Cullen, Jean Toomer, Zora Neale Hurston, George Schuyler, Arna Bontemps, and Langston Hughes. James Weldon Johnson, the poet, wrote: "Have you ever stopped to think what the future Harlem will be? It will be the greatest Negro city in the world!"

Music flourished with Prohibition in innumerable cafés and cabarets, most notably at the Cotton Club, where Duke Ellington played to whites-only audiences who came slumming to Harlem to hear his "jungle music." Black musicians like James P. Johnson, Willie "The Lion" Smith, and Ellington created a new jazz style for Harlem with New York Stride piano. *Vanity Fair* looked at all this and proclaimed that the Negro was "in the ascendancy."

Somebody forgot to tell ordinary African-Americans, who could get only the most menial jobs – porters or washerwomen or office sweeps. Exorbitant rent ate up almost half of their pathetic pay. Most of the landlords were still white. Though real estate brokers made up the largest single black professional group in Harlem's 1930 census, blacks still owned only 6 percent of the property there.

Half of Harlem's black women were part of what *The Crisis*, the NAACP journal, called the "Bronx slave market," laboring as domestics for white families, with little or no pay. About half of the families were on public assistance. "Fully 10,000 . . . now live in cellars: dark, damp, cold dungeons," wrote the Reverend Adam Clayton Powell, Sr., of the Abyssinian Baptist Church. "Here they exist in squalor worse than that of the sharecroppers." Disease was rampant. In Harlem, women giving birth died at twice the rate of the rest of the city. The infant mortality disparity was almost as great. Undertaking became the most profitable business in Harlem.

Of this festering, teeming, ravaged community, Bontemps wrote in 1943: "No matter what else one might see there,

Harlem remained what it had always been in essence: a black ghetto and slum, a clot in the American bloodstream."

When Dr. Collyer moved out of the house on Fifth Avenue in 1919, the black population of Harlem was about 70 percent greater than when he had brought his family there. Black Harlem began only two blocks farther north in houses exactly like the Collyers'. Landlords chopped the spacious old town houses into six and seven one-room flats overflowing with people.

Dr. Collyer's sons lived with their mother in an increasingly isolated vacuum, apparently oblivious to the changing world around them. The Collyer home gradually filled with junk while the town houses around it were broken up into tiny apartments. Langley took his mother downtown to the opera and Homer practiced law on Wall Street. The family lived as if it were still 1899, when Harlem was exclusively white.

The brothers accepted change as long as it was outside their brownstone walls. Langley ranted a bit at the black kids who stoned his windows, yet he chatted occasionally with his new neighbors on the front stoop. He was distant, but gentlemanly. And his neighbors treated him with a kind of bemused deference. They called him Mr. Langley.

After Dr. Collyer moved, he still visited Harlem every day to see "the boys." Or the boys – then in their thirties – visited him at his office in the house on the Upper West Side.

"There was nothing wrong between Uncle Herman and Aunt Susie," said George W. Collyer, Herman's nephew. He popped up to help look for Langley after Homer was found dead. "It was just that she didn't want anything to do with the medical world."

One of the doctor's former patients told Helen Worden: "Even then they wore old-fashioned clothes and looked funny. I remember Homer – young though he was – had a long black beard. Both he and Langley were bright, almost too bright."

That's what their father thought, too. But he and his sons were a lot alike.

Herman's patient found a tremendous amount of "junk" in the basement when she bought the house after his death, including the Model T Ford, which Langley carted away piece by piece.

No blacks lived on the Collyers' block in Harlem when the doctor left. But by the time Susie died in 1929, black Harlem had almost reached 110th Street, its Central Park boundary. And the boys began their retreat into a hermitage of their own creation.

Chapter 7
Arthurian Legend

Uncle Arthur was well on his way to building his own hermitage when I first visited his apartment in the aged tenement on Morris Avenue in the Bronx.

I was eight and it was a totally unwelcoming, grimy brick-and-brownstone building streaked with dirt and even blacker than the rest of the decaying block. It looked worse yet when I came back sixteen years later to help Uncle Arthur move his stuff out.

The tenement was old in 1938 when Uncle Arthur, Uncle Danny, and my grandmother Fannie Lidz moved there from Harlem. "There was a midget woman living over us," Uncle Arthur says. "The mop she had must have been too big. Believe it or not, every time she cleaned the floor, our ceiling rained."

Uncle Arthur gradually filled the sopping apartment with his collections. Grandma died there in 1953 and the bed she died in slowly subsided into his precious junk. My uncles lived on in the apartment until the building was condemned, with Uncle Arthur's treasured hoard still inside.

The condemnation didn't bother Uncle Arthur. He might have stayed on as the conservator of his sidewalk curiosa as the building crumbled around him. But a robber stabbed Uncle Danny just as he stepped into the vestibule of their sixth-floor walk-up. The knife narrowly missed Uncle Danny's heart, he spent six months in a hospital, and he refused to return to the apartment. For once, my paranoid uncle really *had* been followed.

He and Uncle Arthur moved into an SRO hotel on Twenty-first Street in Manhattan. They were slipping back toward their beginnings on the Lower East Side, when all five brothers shared one room with their mother and father.

They were both messengers on Wall Street. Uncle Danny, a Columbia grad not unlike Homer the Scrivener, got Uncle Arthur the job and doubled his salary.

Uncle Arthur had worked for seven years at a dental lab on Union Square. He made impressions and delivered teeth.

"Did the molds ever break?" I asked.

"Well, no," he said. "Sometimes they fell on the floor and my boss said, 'Arthur, come over here and help me look for teeth.'"

He started at eighteen dollars a week in 1965 and was making only forty dollars a week when he left in 1973 to become a messenger.

"One particular guy, the gold-tooth guy, sometimes asked me to sweep the floor after work. He never gave me a cent for that, so one time I got angry and I took his coffee cup and ground a hole it in. He knew it was me.

"Believe it or not, before I left the gold-tooth guy threw me a party," he said. "He even handed me a big jar of cracked teeth and let me have whatever I wanted."

Uncle Arthur made friends with the freight-elevator operator, who offered him basement storage space for his accumulations in the Bronx.

So in the winter of 1974, Uncle Arthur called me – collect, of course – at college in Maryland to come help sneak some of his junk out of the apartment. He said his best stuff was still there.

Uncle Arthur didn't invite my father. Five years before, my dad had stormed the junk castle like some Galahad of Garbage. Uncle Danny had called him in a panic: The superintendent had said that if the junk wasn't moved out, the Lidz brothers would be kicked out. Uncle Arthur thought the super was bluffing, and refused to cooperate. So my father drove from Massachusetts to help out. I came, too.

My father, the last flowering of a generation of Freudians, claimed Uncle Arthur's hoarding was rooted in the "severe repression" of early toilet training. If collectors lose any of their collection, he told me, they lose a part of their identity. He insisted that collecting was Uncle Arthur's way of "channeling aggression and sublimating it." He ignored the fact he was toilet trained by Fannie, too.

There *was* perhaps a defensiveness behind Uncle Arthur's hobby. Like Langley, he built barricades and set booby traps. He nested inside his walls of junk. But he was and remains incapable of aggression. The only time Uncle Arthur really got mad was when my father told him to give it up. The tiny folds that lined his pale forehead were merely the result of squinting down at the sidewalk, not engraved by anger.

But he was angry that day in 1969 when my father arrived to deaccession part of the collection. While my dad lugged armloads of stuff down to the basement incinerator, Uncle Arthur lugged armloads to one of the bedrooms. It was comical, but Uncle Arthur wasn't laughing. Tears pooled in his eyes. I was torn – it got so painful that after an hour or so *I* refused to cooperate. Though my dad plugged on with renewed purpose, at the end of the day he had hardly made a dent in the debris. Incensed, Uncle Arthur told my father never to come back. He never did.

On this bitterly cold evening in 1974, Uncle Arthur and I stood outside on the sidewalk under the tall trees that kept the apartment in perpetual shadow.

"It's a shame they're gonna tear this place down," Uncle Arthur said. "It's part of Bronx history, same as Yankee Stadium."

He had a point.

The tenement might not quite have qualified as a historic edifice as defined by the Colonial Dames of America. The vinyl couches and mirrored décor of the lobby, in fact, suggested a motel bar in Zanesville, Ohio. But in the folk history of the Lidz family, the building had earned landmark status second only to the railroad flat at 98 Orchard Street in which Uncle Arthur and his brothers were born.

The neighborhood was now disintegrating into rubble like a city bombed out during some forgotten war.

In the twilight, pimps on the street corners mumbled, "*Checkitout, checkitout, checkitout.*" Women in short shorts got in and out of cabs. Men prowled in buddy packs like old soldiers who had shared occupation duty. Nightfall flashed hot and jittery, full of frenetic longing that never seemed fulfilled.

Along Morris Avenue, bars, bodegas, and stand-up pizza

joints were strung out like plastic pearls on a dime-store necklace. Street people lounged, lost and passive, the homeless poor, the crippled, the sick, and the mad – dozens on a raw, numbing night. One man lying facedown in a little courtyard might have been dead. Uncle Arthur said he was. He's memorialized in a way, I suppose, in my memory. The dead create their own memorials.

Uncle Arthur and Uncle Danny had lived at 2066 Morris Avenue for thirty-seven years. They'd come from Harlem.

In 1931, the Lidzes had moved to 130th Street so my Uncle Leo could be close to the Harlem branch of City College of New York. He was the family intellectual, a dreamy thinker who wrote hundreds of poems. He favored the Petrarchan sonnet.

He wrote about City College at night. He wrote about Mount Morris Park, a few blocks south of the Collyer mansion.

Where are your brains my men
That you sit there and play cards
Dull eyes dark eyes pale eyes smart eyes
You talk of hearts and clubs and queens
And kings (useless things)

Where are your brains my men
You mingle blacks and whites different types
Some day I hope you will arise
See the light of Brotherhood
And change your state of sordid suffering.

Uncle Leo wrote love poems to half a dozen women. He wrote about a Hindu he met on the subway. And in 1932 he wrote "The Paperhanger's Lament" about the only job he ever had.

My father still remembered the chorus when Uncle Leo died in 1966. He recited it at his funeral.

Crazy rhymes crazy jobs
Crazy World crazy slobs,
Workingmen rats dirty pigs
Lice and Mice and gnats and prigs
Toothless hags hatless giggs,
Join the dance of borrowed wigs.

Uncle Leo failed to fulfil his promise. He went mad in 1935 and attacked his mother with a carving knife. My father had to wrench it from his hand. Uncle Leo was taken away in a straitjacket. He was just thirty when he had his crack-up. He spent the rest of his life in insane asylums.

My father was shattered. He was eighteen and had idolized the older brother who taught him to rhyme and wrestle and quote Rabelais.

The boys were spinning away from their mother. They'd been inseparable since 1920 when her husband, Simon, died in the influenza epidemic. Uncle Harry, the middle son and inspiration for Uncle Leo's couplet "Whose love for justice is unbounded, / Because on Socialism founded," left Harlem to open a leftist bookstore in Chicago. He married a dancer named Diane there.

My father, Sidney, the baby brother, was just nineteen when he married his first wife, Ruth.

"When Sid first married they said they'd never leave us," my grandmother wrote in a journal she kept briefly in 1938. "But as soon as his job seemed to be getting steady, Ruth began bothering him and all of us that she wants her privacy. She began nagging us so, that much against our will, we had to let them go."

You could see where a young bride might be unnerved living with my father's two nutty brothers and a nagging mother-in-law. She and my father moved into a flat on 181st Street, where they lived until my father enlisted in the navy in 1941. He returned from his hitch in 1945 to find Ruth living with somebody else. He divorced her in 1946, and married my mother four years later.

My mother always said Fannie drove her sons crazy. Fannie was possessive and demanding, but inflating her into the mother of all craziness sounds like infantile Freudianism. Until the feminist revolution of the 1960s, whenever the boys went bad, Mom took the fall.

Uncle Danny, the eldest son, left his mother only when he was drafted during World War II – at age forty. And returned home the day after he was discharged. Arthur, a year older than my father, left Fannie for just one month during her lifetime. He went out to a farm in Westchester County and learned how to milk a cow and cut a chicken's throat in the kosher manner, skills he's still proud of.

"The farmer was stingy and sometimes all I had to eat was chicken feed," he recalls. "It wasn't bad. It tasted okay."

On the farm, Uncle Arthur limited his collecting to fireflies and his wrath to the snoopy sharecropper in his bunkhouse. "He used to go through my drawer and touch my stuff," says Uncle Arthur. "So one day I caught some fire bugs and hid them inside the drawer. That night he opened the drawer and saw them light up and screamed. Believe it or not, he never touched my stuff again."

Uncle Arthur and I recovered Fannie's journal in 1974 while rescuing his archives from the Bronx apartment. We'd pushed into the condemned building through the lobby, a burned-out shell that smelled of urine and decay. We followed our flashlight beams, picking our way through the scattered debris to the sixth-floor flat, not unlike Sergeant John Collins following Langley to Homer on his pallet in 1942.

When we opened the door a deadfall of pots and pans clattered to the floor. Uncle Arthur had booby-trapped the entrance much as Langley had in the ghosty house.

The apartment was full of moods and shadows, its endless rolling hills of trash pierced by crannies and unexpected passageways. "I know where everything is, the good stuff and the bad," said Uncle Arthur. "It's like I'm protecting it. The valuable stuff is in a closet way down at the end, under lots of junk. If I can't get to it, how can burglars?"

Uncle Arthur burrowed from tunnel to tunnel like a clever and tenacious rodent. He promised me he'd find Uncle Leo's poems. He emerged with my grandmother's journal, Harry's ninth-grade rhetoric and composition notebook, and wonderful sketches of Harlem drawn by Uncle Leo, but none of his poems. I had to wait twenty-five years to see *them*. Meanwhile, the sketches were lost.

Uncle Leo drew kids in parks and streetscapes of the wide boulevards and churches and familiar vistas. But he also sketched the plain, anonymous brownstones that evoked Harlem's shape and tone and, perhaps, soul. I wonder now if he ever drew the Collyer house.

His drawings mostly caught a specific moment in the history of Harlem. They were all dated, and often he noted the time he drew them. On March 17, 1931, he sketched a three-story storefront house standing alone on Amsterdam Avenue. "Something funny happened that day," he wrote. "They came along and planted a tree in front of me while I was sketching."

He added a note to the picture eight months later: "On Nov. 29, 1931, I observed this building demolished."

His record that the house had red bricks and a brownish-gray cornice was a kind of testament.

Twilight turned into night on Morris Avenue and I grew uneasy. Small sounds rustled through the apartment. Roaches scattered from the circle of my flashlight beam.

Uncle Arthur kicked at a greasy piece of paper under the sink.

"The grease is from tuna fish," he said. "Rats love tuna, so I put some out for them mixed with broken glass from one of my soda bottles. A whole bottle. They ate it up, glass and all. It don't seem to bother those rats."

Uncle Arthur homed in unerringly on a chest-high pile of junk. He pulled forth his lists, one noting dollar bills found and their special characteristics, some torn in half, some with messages, like "Impeach Nixon" and "In Your Guts, You Know He's Nuts." A "dream box" stored bank receipts that had Arthur's dreams recorded on the back.

"I dream of shoelaces," he said.

He loaded his hopes and dreams into two shopping bags and we went downtown on the subway.

I read my grandmother's journal. She wrote in a schoolkid's composition book Uncle Arthur had patched with Band-Aids to keep the binding in place. Her handwriting was bold and clear with special flourishes on the capitals.

"Most of the year 1935 was a very bad one for this family," she wrote, kvetching, *"Leo became sick, I underwent an abdominal operation, and in December I received a disconsolate letter from Diane that Harry was sick. Well, I moped along and must have worried more than I knew because I soon became sick with grief over the two boys, Leo and Harry, and I*

*suffered a nervous breakdown. This lasted until Diane assured
me Harry was OK again and even working. That was in May
1936."*

A year later Uncle Harry stopped by the Harlem apartment
ostensibly on the way to a new job in Philadelphia.

*"He had a friend with him who said he was going to teach
Harry the ropes. For the next six months no news and when I
dunned Art and Dan about it they evaded the issue.*

*"Then Sid and Ruth received a photo of Harry from Mexico
in uniform, and when I said that looked to me like a soldier's
outfit, they said that's how the Mexicans dress.*

*"It seemed strange to me, but like a coward, I was afraid of
the awful truth!*

*"Well, one day I went to put a sandwich in Dan's coat
pocket and out fell a letter. As I stooped to the floor to
pick it up, I could see Harry's writing, and like a hot flame
the words scorched me. 'Spain, artillery, does Ma know
yet?'"*

Uncle Harry had volunteered to fight fascism in the Spanish
Civil War with the Abraham Lincoln Brigade. He was a kid
with a social conscience who got arrested when he was
seventeen, demonstrating against the Japanese invasion of
Manchuria in 1930. By 1937, he had helped organize an early

teamsters union, led a disastrous strike, and opened the socialist bookstore.

He reached Spain in May, and became a courier, sneaking in and out of trenches at the battle of Fuentes de Ebro. "I got promoted to captain in July," he wrote home. "An officer in my battalion got killed. Promotions are rapid and instantaneous. There aren't a lot of candidates."

Uncle Harry fought at Mas de Las Matas, Teruel, the Retreats and the Recrossing of the Ebro, a litany that reads like an elegy from Ernest Hemingway's novel of the war, *For Whom the Bell Tolls*.

His infrequent letters stopped entirely at the end of 1937 when the war turned bad for the loyalists. Of the thirty-two hundred Americans who fought in Spain, only seventeen hundred returned alive. Uncle Harry came back shell-shocked during the summer of 1938. He was sent to a sanatorium in upstate New York. And my grandmother's journals turn to talk of visiting Harry with his wife and my uncles and my father and his wife and various in-laws, and complicated accounts of endless quarreling. She ends one account "And so a good time was had by *none*."

She spent a week near Harry's sanatorium at a place called Millard Lodge.

"I had a nice quiet time. The only excitement was when I saw 'You Can't Take It With You' at the movies. This picture is the grandest, most unique I ever witnessed."

She had to like it, I thought. It's a picture about a family no more loony than the Lidzes, but a whole lot more lovable.

She began to cut off contact with her brothers and sisters. She scoffed at a forty-dollars-a-couple wedding reception at the Hotel Pierre for one of her sisters' daughters.

"I think I would choke eating a $20 luncheon when I find it so hard to pay our $28 rental. I told the girls it would be more mitzvah if they donated the $6,000 the bride was spending on her 300 guests for an ambulance for Spain."

She and her boys Danny and Arthur were becoming more and more isolated in a tiny world of their own hardly bigger than the apartment.

Even my father was becoming neglectful. He still helped support the family. When he and Ruth were newlyweds, they told Fannie not to worry. They said they'd bring her seven dollars every week, enough to pay the rent.

"They really did bring $3 a week for a little while," she wrote, *"then Ruth pleaded they couldn't afford it, although*

Sid was, and is, making more than ever. So for the past year they haven't helped at all. And now it seems they are conferring a special favor if they come to see us.

  "Such is life."

Chapter 8
Just a Greater Walk with Thee

Helen Worden knew she had a great story after she talked to Langley Collyer, but her editor said she needed a peg to hang it on. When a real estate agent from Queens turned up with a deal for the Collyers she had her hook. She broke her story on August 11, 1938, and shattered their decade of reclusive silence.

Maurice Gruber had been haunting the house for six weeks with an offer for nine acres of land the Collyers owned on Long Island that had been assessed at $125,000. Herman Collyer had bought the tract as an investment in 1870. Homer and Langley had played on it as boys, but hadn't seen it for half a century.

Gruber never got closer to the brothers than banging on their drainpipe. But Worden was more interested in working her story than in his deal. She retailed every rumor in Harlem.

"He has a Model T Ford in the basement."

"He carries his money in a carpetbag."

"He doesn't believe in banks . . ."

"He owns half of New York's waterfront."

The next day she opened her story, asking a decade prematurely: "Is Homer Collyer dead?"

On the third day, Langley told a *Journal-American* reporter, "I want to say most emphatically the current stories in the newspapers are just tommyrot!"

"Rich?" he said. "I'll do well to pay my taxes this year."

"A carpetbag? I never even saw one!"

"I don't believe in banks, and keep all my money in the house? In the first place, my money consists of only a very few dollars, all of which I keep in a bank."

"Own half of the waterfront? My total property consists of my home, the house across the street, and a small piece of land in Long Island!"

"An old car and a boat in my house? Asinine and ridiculous."

He wasn't quite truthful. Police found the canoe and the Model T when they found Homer.

The *Journal-American* dubbed them the "Hermits of Harlem." From now on, the Collyer brothers would measure out their lives in column inches of newspaper type.

Six weeks after Worden wrote her first story, a burglar broke into the boarded-up house at 2077 Fifth. Nothing was taken. There was nothing to take. Langley was more upset at the police and reporters, the *Journal* noted, than at "the fruitless foray of the burglars."

The Con Ed men shoved them into the headlines again in 1939 when they poked Langley in the belly while taking out the gas meters.

"Most folks say Langley is a bit touched," wrote Harold Conrad, the *Gotham Grapevine* columnist. "But Langley takes the papers home and reads the foreboding headlines. He thinks most folks are touched. We wonder who is right."

The next great assault on the Collyer hermitage came in the summer of 1942 when they were threatened with eviction from their brownstone bastion.

Helen Worden got a tip from the corner druggist, Jacob Iglitzen, who said a dispossess notice had been nailed to the door at 2078 Fifth Avenue. The Collyers were ordered to court to show cause why they should not be evicted. The Bowery Savings Bank foreclosed the mortgage and took title on July 23. The brothers hadn't paid the bank for eleven years. They owed sixty-seven hundred dollars.

"When did you last see Langley?" Worden asked the druggist.

"Only the other night," Iglitzen said. "He was standing on the corner of 125th and Fifth Avenue chewing on a crust of bread. He greeted me politely enough, folded the bit of crust into a bread wrapper, and explained he was on his way to market. I invited him into a restaurant for a bowl of soup. But he declined. He had quite a bit of shopping to do."

Iglitzen said Langley was making his rounds in his usual rags and dragging his customary cardboard box by a rope.

"His face looked freshly washed, but he was a mess otherwise."

Iglitzen asked about Homer.

"Homer's fine," Langley had told him. "But he's getting tired of lying on his back. I will have to turn him soon. And that is quite a task."

A *Herald Tribune* reporter named Herbert Clyde Lewis was staked out at the mansion the next day about ten-thirty P.M.

"It was mugging time in Harlem," he wrote. "The reporter's nerves were on edge."

The door creaked open and Langley Collyer appeared out of the darkness at the top of the front steps. He carefully locked up and turned, stroking his gray mustache. He looked "for all the world like an old Chinese Mandarin who had come upon hard times."

"I'm going to the bakery to buy some buns for my brother,"

Langley said. "If you care to walk along with me I wouldn't mind. I can't go out until late at night, when my brother, Homer, is ready to go to sleep. But he's all right now. He's listening to music over the radio."

He set out, dragging his cardboard box behind, Lewis tagging along, unfortunately wearing a brand-new pair of shoes he'd bought only a few hours earlier.

"Mr. Collyer walked and walked," Lewis complained. "He walked along 125th Street to Lenox Avenue. He walked down Lenox Avenue to 110th Street. He walked to Central Park West, and downtown toward Times Square."

Langley was aware of the Collyer mythos.

"The superstitious people say we live in a haunted house," he said. "They say I barricade the window and double-bolt the doors because my brother is dead inside and I'm afraid to let the police in.

"The truth is that I barricade the windows to keep thieves out. I have put boxes all over the house, so that if thieves break in they will trip in the darkness and I will hear them.

"The people in the neighborhood have tormented and abused us for years. The children have broken more than two hundred windows, and finally I stopped replacing them and boarded them up instead."

He loped along, Lewis said, toting his old carton, unmindful of the stares of passersby. He turned down a cigarette. Never had a smoke or drink in his life, he said.

Langley explained that he and his brother wanted to live their lives their own way. They had no phone because "Homer can't lift himself out of bed to answer, and there's no one in particular I want to talk to."

The reporter's new shoes were now biting into his arches. He suggested a tour of the *Herald Tribune* Building on West Forty-first Street.

"I'd be delighted," Langley said. "It isn't often I can get out. I don't like to leave my brother alone . . .

"I'd like to see your machinery," he said. "I've always been interested in machinery. Is there anything strange about that? Can you call a man strange as my neighbors do, because I like to tinker with machinery?"

"No," Lewis said. He whistled for a cab.

"Don't take a cab. It's a waste of money!"

They toured the paper. Homer had his picture taken in the photo department holding a big old portrait camera. He expounded on printing in the composing room. The whirling presses fascinated him.

Lewis packed him into a cab about two A.M. for the

ride home. "I'd like to come in and meet Homer," he said.

"Please excuse me, but I'm ashamed to ask you in," Langley said. "The house is too upset, all those thousands of newspapers and all those pianos . . ."

When they pulled up in front of the darkened house at 128th Street, he said, "Don't be alarmed by these old clothes I wear. Dressed like this, no one ever molests me. I have seen people held up under this old elm tree. I've peered out at night from the shutters and seen them stabbed and robbed."

He stepped from the cab and picked up scraps of paper and broken glass from the front yard.

"It's the same every night," he complained, "Always rubbish in the yard. I can't do the work of fifteen or twenty men, though I'd like to."

He fumbled for his keys.

"It's been a pleasant evening," he said. "I never did get to the bakery, but I can go some other time. It isn't often I meet congenial people. I've neglected my social life badly."

Chapter 9

The Citadel Saved

"I hope something can be done at the bank about the eviction," Langley told Lewis. "Homer doesn't know anything about it. It would be the death of him if he found out, I'm sure. I can't tell him and yet I have to tell him someday because he handles all our financial affairs. The reason we're in a bit of trouble is that Homer is paralyzed and can't move his hand to sign any papers."

The notices vanished from the door the next day. About a week later Langley made an unprecedented appearance in broad daylight. He walked eight miles downtown to McMullen's law office on Park Row. By the time he had walked the eight miles back, it was dark. A sizable crowd of his neighbors had gathered, trading rumors while they awaited him.

"There are five coffins in the basement."

"Langley hauls dead bodies through a tunnel in the street to his other house yonder."

A boy shouted, "Mr. Langley's coming down the avenue." The crowd pushed to the corner.

"We're with you, Mr. Collyer!" they cried. "We won't let them evict you. We're your friends."

Worden recalled he stood in a circle of light from a streetlamp. He wore a black suit, a high white collar, a noticeably clean white shirt, Congress gaiters, and a flowing silk Windsor tie. Worden noticed his shoes were dusty after his sixteen-mile hike.

"I appreciate your kind words," he told the crowd. "It's nice to know that we have some friends. If some of you could only tell the younger element to stop breaking our windows and littering our yard with junk, I'd be very appreciative."

A local air-raid warden, Ann Emmett, suggested that if he and Homer needed money to keep eviction at bay he could give a piano concert at the Harlem Boys Club. Langley asked what kind of piano the club had. "A baby grand," Emmett said. Nodding approvingly, Langley asked her to write him a letter – "Not special delivery" – and he'd consider the proposal.

The crowd wanted to know where Homer was.

"My brother is not well enough to receive guests," Langley said. "He lies there, eyes closed, but he never sleeps. Often he talks in the middle of the night. I write down everything he says. It is worthwhile. He has invented a marvelous telescope."

You could pay off the mortgage with that, someone suggested.

"No, so far the ideas are only in Homer's mind."

McMullen put off their eviction by the bank with an offer to repurchase the house. But for the next six weeks the brothers left his letters unopened. Then, to comply with a health-department order, the bank sent around a crew to clean up the property. The bank declared itself "exasperated."

"Langley has gone too far," said F. Donald Richart, a vice president. "We will clean the yard and we will reluctantly put Mr. Langley out."

At the end of September, a crew led by Mrs. Pauline Farkas began removing a fence on the 128th Street side of the house.

Langley opened the shutters and leaned out of a second-floor window, shouting, "Police! Police! That's my property. You've got no right to break into my property."

Mrs. Farkas shouted up: "The bank told me to clean this up."

"The bank has nothing to do with this," Langley said. "I'm the owner. Don't steal that property."

A huge crowd was on the corner, rooting for the Collyers,

when the first police cars rolled up. This day's rumor was that the bank was going to board up the house so tight, the brothers would be forced out for want of air. "When we got there, there were about five hundred people, making a lot of noise – you know, kidding around," said patrolman Timothy Shannon. "We asked the woman to show her order and she didn't have it, so we told her to stop."

Mrs. Farkas decamped.

"I didn't know there were any people living in there," she later said, still unnerved. "I told them I didn't want to travel in Harlem. There's always excitement up there."

She stayed home and sent her husband, Joe, the next day, which was even more exciting.

Two kids pulled a fire alarm, bringing a dozen police cars and fire trucks. The construction crew showed up in a truck and a car. A delegation of four bankers arrived. Two insurance agents followed. Brandishing a court order, Joe Farkas brought up the rear. The crowd was as big as the day before.

"There he is," a voice shouted.

Langley ran from window to window as workmen moved junk from his weedy yard: rusted metal, cracked egg crates, rotting doors.

"Leave those doors alone," he bellowed. "They're mine. I

want those slabs of marble. I defy anybody to take what belongs to me. Officer, Officer, stop them. I didn't know a human being could be so persecuted.

"I say, I need those doors to prevent people from breaking in here. How can we keep thieves out of here, Officer, if they take those doors?"

McMullen arrived around noon. He found the mailbox jammed with letters. The city owed the Collyers $856.12. Two banks were trying frantically to have Homer withdraw more than three thousand dollars from long-dormant accounts.

"They have asked me to tell him by mail that if he will only sign an X to the release form in Langley's presence they will be glad to give the money to Langley if he calls at the banks," said McMullen. That was about as likely to happen as a return engagement at Camegie Hall.

Another $22,500 in uncollected rent awaited the Collyers for billboards posted for fifteen years along their property in Long Island.

But Bowery Savings did not get paid. Langley retreated to the silence of his inner sanctum. The bank and its goons withdrew in frustration.

They returned with an even greater force in November, determined to evict the Collyers. A full phalanx of reporters, photographers, and newsreel crews arrived with them. The Collyers were front-page news.

The bank's eviction brigade included a banker, three lawyers from Cadwalder, Wickersham & Taft, seven workmen, a sheriff and two deputies, three marshals, a hook-and-ladder crew from the fire department, two radio cars full of cops, a physician, and a seventy-two-year-old locksmith named Joseph Cohen.

Bowery Savings offered to move the Collyers to their house across the street or put them up. The bank even had an ambulance standing by in case Homer needed hospitalization. It's unclear if the paramedics brought any oranges.

McMullen knocked. No answer. "Langley!" he yelled. No answer.

The sheriff nodded to the firemen. They hotfooted it into the areaway and raised ladders to the parlor-floor windows.

"A wall of newspapers and rubble made the windows impenetrable," Worden reported.

" 'Use your hatchets, boys,' the marshal called. 'And what about the locksmith taking a try at the storm door?' "

Cohen attacked the massive mahogany door with hammer, chisel, and crowbar. He smashed the lock and opened the door. A twelve-foot-high pile of debris reinforced with wire netting confronted him. And there was another barricade of junk beyond.

He went to the basement and ripped off the iron grille. Another pile of rubbish, even bigger, and another door. Cohen went to the back door, broke it down, and was stopped by a sheet-metal door. He tried another door in the backyard. It came off easily and he found himself standing in a small walled-in cubicle that had once been a servant's privy.

In desperation, Cohen and the sheriffs returned to the front entrance. A crowd of one thousand, many cheering schoolkids at recess, watched Cohen break in a front window and shimmy headfirst into the funereal darkness.

His son became worried: "Hey, Pop. Where the hell are you?"

Only echoes.

A deputy sheriff, in a new topcoat and neatly pressed trousers, went in after Papa Cohen. A funnel of dust billowed from the open window. A few minutes later the deputy reappeared at the window, smudged with dirt and covered in cobwebs.

"This is a hell of a mess," he gasped. "Every place we go is filled with rubbish. I can't even get to the front door."

The sheriff called for reinforcements.

"There's nothing to do but tunnel through to the hall," a deputy said.

Worden said that in three hours they had gone less than two feet into the drawing room. "The trash is like quicksilver," Cohen told her. "When you step into it, you step into space. I know our boys are in that room, but I can't find them." By noon the crew emerged from their tunnel exhausted, caked with the dust of years – and hungry.

"At this rate it will take weeks to evict the Collyers," a Bowery banker said to Cohen.

"You're darned right," said Cohen. "If you gave me a thousand dollars I wouldn't carry on this job after today. The rats have scared me."

He cut short the assault on the junk by taking the storm doors off their hinges. Cops clambered in over boxes and barrels and crates stacked in the foyer to the second floor.

"Mr. McMullen! Mr. McMullen!" Langley cried in a weak voice from behind one of his pianos.

With the help of police and firemen, the elderly and long-suffering lawyer climbed a ladder and crawled through a tunnel to the belly of the fortress.

"I've been sick for a number of days and couldn't attend to affairs," Langley said from his lair behind the piano. "Homer had a fainting spell while the rumpus was going on. We're both sick, but won't have any doctor, if you please."

McMullen insisted Langley had to pay the bank sixty-seven hundred dollars or be evicted.

"Here's the sixty-seven hundred dollars," Langley said. He waved a roll of bills above the piano like a white flag of surrender.

The bankers and their lawyers retired. The firemen and police withdrew. Workmen shuttered the windows and replaced the doors. The crowd dispersed. The Collyers had persevered in their dark castle.

The Collyers' next photo finish with the law came only two months later. Homer had stopped paying income taxes in 1931. Langley probably never earned an income to tax in his whole life. In January 1943, the federal government decided Homer owed nineteen hundred dollars. Tax agents threatened to seize their house across the street, at 2077 Fifth Avenue. McMullen thought they might settle.

"Of course," he said, "it's impossible to tell what they'll do. I've not been able to speak to Langley since he paid off the Bowery Savings Bank. I've written him dozens of letters but we've not had a reply."

With the aid of police, McMullen arranged a code – he'd

blow his car horn three times at a given hour and wait for Langley to come to his car.

The brothers still had thousands of dollars in unclaimed savings accounts, some opened by their mother years before.

"I raised the question of taxes and bank accounts," Jacob Iglitzen told Worden. "But Langley said he didn't feel in the mood to discuss business."

The government ordered the house at 2077 auctioned off in February. Nobody bid. The government had to buy the property for one hundred dollars, the minimum set by the auctioneer. In December 1944, the taxmen offered to sell the property back to Homer. The blind man turned a deaf ear.

"He is not a foolish man," said McMullen. He'd owe the city five thousand dollars in back property taxes. The *New York Sun* trumpeted: HOMER COLLYER TOUTED AS U.S. NO. 1 TAX PAIN.

The brothers not only ignored the income-tax agents, they never registered for the draft in World War II or applied for ration stamps needed for sugar and meat. They remained oblivious when the Harlem race riots of August 1943 erupted around them.

The upheavals began when a white policeman tried to arrest a black woman in a dispute between her and a hotel keeper. He wounded a black soldier who tried to intervene. Word spread that a white cop had shot and killed a black GI. Thousands took to the streets, businesses were looted, cars overturned, police and firemen stoned. The rioting lasted through the night and into the next morning. Hundreds were arrested and hundreds more injured, some clubbed and shot by police. Six people died.

The Collyers acknowledged their surroundings again only in June 1946 when police found two intruders stripping the plumbing. One got away, the other, a homeless man, was arrested. Even then Langley had to be subpoenaed to appear in court.

Langley turned up in high style, wearing a high-buttoned blue serge suit, a white shirt turned inside out, and a flowing Windsor silk bow tie. He told reporters assembled once again for a Collyer yarn that life in Harlem had been "forty years of harassment by hoodlums." He had only seventy-five cents in his pocket – he was afraid of pickpockets and carried only what he needed.

He hadn't voted in years, he said, and didn't care about politics, just science. After all, he did have degrees in chemistry and mechanical engineering. He recalled hearing the news of the atom bomb on his crystal radio.

"I thought then that the atomic bomb was just a fanciful name. I don't believe it works by breaking down the atom. The method is just a more rapid release of nitrogen gas."

On his rare subway ride downtown, he had collected a neat bundle of newspapers to add to his stock of back issues for Homer, whose health was improving and who might soon regain his sight.

"I cook all his food for him," he said once again. "And he's never had indigestion." Homer, he said, weighed two hundred pounds and was in great shape. "I treat him myself – we've never had a doctor. We don't believe in drugs and such things." He did believe in physical culture and calisthenics and massage. "I've lost fifty pounds in that time because I have never slept, but I'm not complaining. I have a way of relaxing without sleeping so I can be ready to answer my brother whenever he needs anything."

Langley remarked that he used to be a concert pianist who had "won ten grand prizes." And though he kept ten grand pianos, he avoided them because they were in "another room. I haven't touched the keys of any of them in a long, long time." He knew twenty-five hundred pieces from memory. He expressed a distaste for the moderns, "even Gershwin."

Despite Langley's rattling on, the burglar was convicted and dispatched to the Tombs.

The brothers were celebrities in spite of themselves. They made news without ever trying. In November, a *Sun* headline read RECLUSES CALM DESPITE BLAZE: COLLYER BROTHERS SHOW NO INTEREST IN FIRE NEXT DOOR.

In January 1947, the city condemned the Long Island property for a street-building project. The *Herald Tribune* attended the condemnation hearing along with the Reverend James L. McCabe, the pastor of St. Benedict the Moor. Reverend McCabe encountered Langley and offered to buy a small parcel for a church building project.

"For the good of your soul now and hereafter," the priest said.

Langley rebuffed him.

"If I wish to make a gift to the church for the repose of my soul," he said, "I'll give cash, not my property."

The next news stories announced Homer's death.

The *Herald Tribune* had already summed the Collyers up pretty well in a 1942 editorial titled "The Nonconformists":

Two brothers – indrawn, sufficient unto each other, leading the
life they chose, following a rationality all their own. Not anti-

social – "We never violate the law" – not misanthropic nor embittered. Simply refusing to take the lead from others; knowing the ways and things of the outside world and rejecting them. "All we want is for people to let us alone," said Langley Collyer, the man of polished manners and of questing mind, devoting his years to quiet service to his blind brother. "A man's home is his castle."

Chapter 10
Uncle Arthur Meets His Match

On August 7, 1975, Uncle Arthur and Uncle Danny signed a lease for a one-bedroom flat in The Argyle, a low-rise Flatbush apartment building just south of Prospect Park. On August 8, they were threatened with eviction. Their new landlord wasn't pleased with the *objets d'junque* Uncle Arthur was already dragging in from Ocean Avenue. In response, Uncle Arthur put eight locks on the door. Just as he had in the Bronx, Uncle Danny lowered the shades. They wouldn't be raised again for another twenty-four years, growing progressively more yellow, then brown.

Once again my uncles had moved to a neighborhood in transition, once again belatedly to the tune of "Theme from *Exodus*." They arrived as their part of Brooklyn shifted in just ten years from about 90 percent Jewish and white to a multiethnic, multicultural area, mostly African-American. Pockets of Orthodox Jews still lived on the western edge of Flatbush. Middle-class whites lived in big wood-frame homes built at the turn of the century on gracious tree-lined streets parallel to Ocean Avenue. A striking example a few blocks from The Argyle is a rambling Queen Anne–style Victorian home, its turrets, peaked gables, and terra-cotta roof as whimsical as a daisy pushing through cracked pavement. Uncle Arthur found these new streets a virgin paradise on trash-collection days.

Uncle Danny died a paranoid's death in 1980 – he had a heart attack while accusing his cardiologist of bugging his pacemaker. A year later my father died of leukemia. In 1983, Uncle Arthur got a new roomie: Uncle Harry, the only other Lidz brother left. He'd been sprung from the asylum in 1978 after forty years and he'd been living alone in Buffalo. Diane had divorced him in 1939, a year after Uncle Harry was certified.

A onetime featherweight boxer who had been knocked out in the first round of his one and only Golden Gloves bout, Uncle Harry was committed to the belief that he was the world amateur boxing champion in nine different weight divisions. He was the founder of the Harry Lidz Worldwide Fan Club, as well as its president in perpetuity.

In the spring of 1983, on his seventieth birthday, I threw

Uncle Harry a party in my Upper West Side apartment. A week later an ad appeared four hundred miles away in the personals column of *The Buffalo News*:

> HARRY LIDZ, Athletics president Harlem,
> 1930–31 retired winner. Thanks his fans
> 1983 for Manhattan party.

Uncle Harry and Uncle Arthur shared the apartment for fifteen years, feuding and bickering like Beckett tramps. Ingenuous Arthur, Combative Harry. Comrades in limbo who couldn't live with or without each other. Uncle Arthur resented Uncle Harry's smoking because it endangered his trash tinderbox; Uncle Harry, a fastidious phantom, resented Uncle Arthur's collecting and made him stuff his junk in plastic bags and the priority-mail envelopes he got free from the post office. "The guy won't listen," complained Uncle Arthur. "No compromise, no compromise. He's gonna do what he wants and that's it."

Unlike the Collyer brothers, the Lidz boys didn't shrink from the limelight. *Unstrung Heroes* had brought a certain notoriety to Uncle Harry and legitimized Uncle Arthur, or at least given him a rationale for collecting. When the book was made into a movie, the director, Diane Keaton, requested to meet them. To her, Uncle Harry and Uncle Arthur were the real celebrities.

I asked my uncles if they'd like to go to Hollywood to watch the filming. "Sure," they chorused, even though Uncle Harry believed an "impostor" would play him, and Uncle Arthur was convinced he would have to pay someone to portray him. "It'll be nice to breathe clean air," said Uncle Arthur, who rarely left New York City and had never left the East Coast. He had been on a plane only once – in 1963 – and that was to visit Uncle Harry's Buffalo sanatorium.

My uncles were waiting outside The Argyle. Uncle Arthur bent down to pick up an empty pack of cigarettes.

"Leave it, Arthur," snapped Uncle Harry.

"For who?" asked Uncle Arthur.

One of their neighbors walked by. She was a pleasant, shapeless woman of great bulk and baleful aspect. "Hello, Harry and Angelo," she said. Though the woman had known Arthur for twenty years, she still called him Angelo. "She comes from an Italian family," Uncle Arthur more or less explained. "You have to have an Italian name."

Endearing and undefended confusion had always been part of Uncle Arthur's character. "There's a lady in my building whose parents came from Sicily," he said in his slow, halting way. "They've been in America fifteen years."

"So the lady was born in Sicily?"

"No, Brooklyn. The same as her older brothers and sisters."

"How many brothers and sisters does the lady have?"

"Five. Including herself."

Futzing with keys and gadgets that he removed from the depths of his baggy trousers, Uncle Arthur opened the door to his apartment. Not a glimmer of light lit the inner hallway as we entered. As he shut the door softly, I squeezed through a passage rendered by the frame of an ancient sewing machine, three folding chairs, broken brooms, parts of a rocking chair, a bedspring, and six-foot-high bales of overnight mailbags, which had become collectibles in themselves.

Like an Arab peddler displaying wares in a souk, Uncle Arthur reached into a mass of newspapers and pulled forth Wagging, his cat.

"Wagging obeys me most of the time," he said, his voice carefully spooning out one word at a time. "She gives me lots of pleasure and bites and scratches. At night, she bangs against my feet for food. When I get dressed in the morning, she lays her head on my shoes. Flies, she goes after on the windowsill. When a fire engine passes, the ears move."

"The flies' ears?" I asked.

"The cat's, the cat's. When I read a newspaper on the table, Wagging jumps up on the table and paws at the paper. She falls asleep in my box of dreams."

Mice scurried across the floor and nibbled on Wagging's food while she watched benignly.

Uncle Harry sat erect on a pile of papers, smoking a Camel, gazing fixedly out the window, a long, gaunt, craggy man of eighty-two with the profile of an eagle. "Want lunch?" he mumbled to the window. He offered me an English muffin that looked as if it had been sitting on the counter since the end of the Reformation. I graciously declined.

Uncle Harry opened the freezer and removed a package of ground beef. It was seven different shades of gray, having been defrosted and refrozen at least as many times.

"You can't do that to meat!" I said.

"What's the worst that could happen?" Uncle Harry sneered.

"You'd die."

"Is *that* all?"

He placed the ground beef on the counter, and the three of us left to buy provisions. When we returned a few hours later, the meat was gone. The kitchen had swallowed it.

My uncles spent the next few days frantically preparing for their trip. They visited the grave of Uncle Leo on Staten Island. They boarded Wagging at an animal shelter. They packed. And unpacked. And packed again. And unpacked again. When it was finally time to leave for the airport, Uncle Harry announced, "I'm not going."

"How come?" asked Uncle Arthur.

"I want my sparring partners with me."

"Who are your sparring partners?" I asked.

"The king of Spain, the king of France, and the king of Philadelphia." He may have meant King of Prussia. Not that it mattered. After four hours of pleading and prodding, he still wouldn't budge. A royal pain was Uncle Harry.

We set off for Los Angeles without him. Uncle Arthur left from New York. I flew out of Philadelphia with my daughters, nine-year-old Gogo and six-year-old Daisy. Though they had never been to Uncle Arthur's apartment, he exerted a magnetic pull on them. They were attracted to his eccentricities – the way he coveted wrapping paper more than gifts – and repelled by his musty clothes and prickly whiskers. They tended to greet him with phantom hugs from five feet away.

We were waiting for Uncle Arthur in the baggage area at LAX when he arrived dressed comfortably in old running shoes, maroon checked polyester trousers that had seen better decades, and a wide silk paisley tie that some stockbroker must have bought on feverish impulse in 1968 to match his wife's Pucci pants. A New York Mets cap of unknown vintage generously covered his twin dikes of silver hair, and black electrician's tape bulged from his glasses. Uncle Arthur lugged two battered valises.

Gogo watched them intently. "Uncle Arthur," she whispered, "what's in the bags?"

"More bags."

Baggies, it turned out, were all Uncle Arthur had brought for his week in California. "To collect in," he explained. He got a good start on the plane, where he bagged five bars of soap, a stack of paper towels and eight airline timetables. "Everything on planes has changed," he marveled. "Now there's phones, TVs—even the sky outside the window is different."

Uncle Arthur mostly wanted to walk around Disneyland. My father, the lapsed socialist, had told him Uncle Walt was a "fascist rat," even bigger than the ones that infested his Bronx apartment. The image was bricked into Uncle Arthur's brain.

So we drove to Anaheim and Uncle Arthur walked. And walked. And walked. We tried to keep up. He walked to Adventureland. He walked through Frontierland. He walked past Tomorrowland. At the entrance to Fantasyland, he walked into a human-size Mickey Mouse.

"What land are you from?" Uncle Arthur said.

Mickey stood mute.

"Where you from?" Uncle Arthur repeated.

Silence.

Uncle Arthur shook his head and muttered, "Mice!"

On the way back to the hotel, Uncle Arthur had me stop at a shoe store. He looked around, inspected a couple of shoes, and lingered at the register. He wanted to buy some yellow laces, but he was a little short on cash. I came up with the change. "How much money did you bring?" I asked.

"About fifty," he said.

"Fifty dollars?"

"Not fifty dollars!" he said dismissively. "Fifty cents."

We drove to Pasadena to see the movie set for Uncle Arthur's apartment. Only traces remained of my book, and the Bronx wasn't one of them. Uncle Arthur had been turned into a compulsive collector of wedding-cake ornaments whose trove of flea-market knickknacks was hygienically boxed and labeled as if in a Hold Everything catalog display. Evidently, the reality of musty cardboard and cockroach-teeming news-print didn't fit the set designer's *Metropolitan Home* aesthetic.

Uncle Arthur sighed when he saw the newspapers in his movie home in tightly drawn bundles. "Looks like Harry's been here," he cracked.

Gogo asked Uncle Arthur if his own junk looked so neat. "Mine don't look like junk," he said. "It looks like a bunch of hobbies all over the floor, in boxes, in grocery bags, in mailbags."

Daisy asked Uncle Arthur if he reshuffled his hobbies or left them in big piles.

"I sort my junk out all the time," he said. "I have stuff in separate bags. I even have bags in separate bags."

Gogo: "Is your junk hard to walk through?"

Uncle Arthur: "I've made paths to walk through my junk. Well, not exactly paths, but enough room to get around. In the living room, the junk comes up to about my chest. In the bedroom, it isn't too bad: It just comes up to my knees."

Daisy: "Is your junk hard to *see* through?"

Uncle Arthur: "I can always see my way around. Unless I crouch."

Gogo: "So what's so good about your junk?"

Uncle Arthur: "I'm used to it. It's interesting, like a book. I have special articles on different subjects, like politics and science. They go back to moon time, when people walked on the moon. There's something new all the time. They're experimenting with people, with animals, with cloning. In case anybody wants any information, I have it for them. It makes me feel important. The trouble is nobody else recognizes how important the stuff I save is."

The next day we drove to an SRO hotel in downtown L.A., where a scene for the film was being shot. Uncle Arthur looked great. Everything about him shined: his pink cheeks, his bald head, his tape-wadded glasses, his scrubbed fingernails, his shoes. "I'm anxious to talk to the other me," he said. "And Diane." Though he had never met Keaton or talked to her or seen her dither as Annie Hall, Uncle Arthur was smitten. He'd written her many letters. She had written a few back. Once, while visiting my house, Uncle Arthur had me rent some of her movies. The one he liked best was *Look Who's Talking Now*, in which she's the voice of a poodle.

"Which character is Diane?" Uncle Arthur kept asking.

"The one with the tail," I kept answering.

Uncle Arthur wagged this around in his head awhile. "She's a pretty good actress," he said at last. "I thought I was watching a real dog."

On our way to the set, I pointed out Keaton's face on a Sunset Boulevard billboard. "Gee whiz," said Uncle Arthur. "What's she doing up there?"

"She's in a TV movie as Amelia Earhart," I said.

"Amelia Earhart's a dog?"

"Not a dog, an aviator," said Gogo, who had just read a book about her.

"Oh . . . I get it," said Uncle Arthur, not getting it.

We pulled into a parking lot in a squalid part of L.A. The four of us wandered around movie trailers, stopping at one marked "Uncle Arthur." Standing in the doorway was Maury Chaykin, a big, burly man with the round, inscrutable face of a Buddha. His frayed gray corduroy jacket had a white carnation in the lapel; his narrow tie, regimental stripes.

"Hi," said Uncle Arthur. "I'm Uncle Arthur."

"Me, too," said Chaykin.

The two Uncle Arthurs instantly hit it off. They strolled down an alley, scrounging for collectibles. Skinny Arthur said: "Remember Hansel and Gretel? They made a trail with sugar crumbs." Fat Arthur said: "Wasn't it bread crumbs?" Skinny Arthur said: "I don't know. It was before my time." Fat Arthur nodded. Skinny Arthur said: "Most people look up. I look down. Believe it or not, you find everything that way." Fat Arthur looked down and found a penny. "Here," he told Skinny. "You can have this."

"No."

"I insist."

"Well . . . all right." Skinny dropped the penny into his pocket. It clanked against the fifty already there.

Gogo and Daisy came running over. "Uncle Arthur," said Daisy excitedly. "How did it feel to meet yourself?"

"The other me is big and stout," he said. "I'm very thin. As far as that goes, there's no resemblance. And his shoes! They're all dirty. That's overdoing it a little, in my opinion."

That day's scene was being shot in the lobby of a seedy hotel. On an overstuffed couch sat Michael Richards, the actor who played Uncle Danny. I introduced him to Uncle Arthur.

"Arthur," said Richards. "What made Danny think the world was persecuting him?"

"What makes you think it wasn't?" said Uncle Arthur.

A woman in a thin and tattered bathrobe – an actual resident of the hotel – sidled up to Uncle Arthur. "You're the only one here who looks authentic," she told him.

"He is authentic," I said.

She handed him a quarter.

Uncle Arthur's face had taken on the worried, wrinkled appearance of a walnut. "Where's Diane?" he asked. The director was down at the lunch wagon, it turned out, getting grilled by Gogo.

"When you played Amelia Earhart," Gogo asked earnestly, "did you learn to fly or were strings attached to you?"

Diane pursed her lips in a charming, bashful smile. She was all in white, her neck was coiled with pearls, her left arm was banded with four wristwatches. Uncle Arthur eyed her watchfully, half expecting her to roll over and play dead. Diane's eyes met Uncle Arthur's. She stepped to one side, and so, as if they were waltzing, did Uncle Arthur. "So, Uncle Arthur," she said. Little groans issued forth.

Uncle Arthur took a deep breath. "Holy gee! Wow! Oh, boy!"

"Well, I mean, like, well, oh well . . ."

"Yeah . . . well . . . gosh . . ."

"So, uh, how do you feel?"

"Like . . . like I'm dreaming."

"Oh, right, oooh, wow!"

Diane sat down. "Sit," she told Uncle Arthur.

Softly: "I will."

Something was weighing heavily on Uncle Arthur. The yellow shoelaces in his pocket. "I was gonna give them to Diane," he confessed on the way back to our hotel. "But I decided to keep them for myself. I hope she won't mind."

"Don't worry," I said. "She'll get over it."

Twilight came down Sunset Boulevard like a long, slow fadeout at the end of a movie, and finally Uncle Arthur's hotel room was dark except for the flickering blue light of a television set. My uncle the collector fell asleep surrounded by plastic bags filled with remnants of his adventures and dreams, a smile of contentment on his face and visions of sugar crumbs dancing in his head.

Chapter 11
Ballyhoo

Homer's death was page-one news fit to print even in *The New York Times*:

HOMER COLLYER, HARLEM RECLUSE, FOUND DEAD AT 70, the staid *Times* reported concisely, if inaccurately, on the Saturday morning after the body was found. Homer was sixty-five.

The *Daily News*, then the epitome of tabloid sensationalism, got his age right for the Sunday paper. They were already looking for an angle with their headline: COLLYER HOME KEEPS LIFE-OR-DEATH SECRET.

The *Post*, less lurid but more liberal than today, had broken the story on Friday, March 21, 1947, the day Homer was found. They stated just the facts: FIND HERMIT DEAD IN SEARCH OF HOME.

The Collyer brothers' story exploded into the last great ballyhoo in that moment before the rise of television when

New York newspapers were ascendant and powerful in a way they'd never be again. A ballyhoo in the twenties and thirties and forties was a spontaneous media extravaganza. There were eight major newspapers in Manhattan and they all wanted their special slice of the Collyer brothers baloney. So did the *Brooklyn Daily Eagle*, the leftist *PM*, *The Catholic Worker*, and the *New Masses*, two African-American weeklies, and a score of foreign-language newspapers. The Collyers made "The Talk of the Town" in *The New Yorker* – twice. *Time* magazine covered them with a two-page feature. *Life* produced its story in a four-page picture-and-prose spread. Most impressively, the brothers rated headlines in the *Bronx Home News*, which demanded a local angle in every story. (When Charles Lindbergh crossed the Atlantic in 1927, the *Home News* trumpeted: LINDBERGH FLIES OVER BRONX ON WAY TO PARIS.)

Three papers clashed in a bidding war for tips about Langley's whereabouts. The *Journal-American* offered $1,000. The *Daily News* promised $1,500. The *Mirror* did the *News* one better, exactly one better – $1,501.

The *Mirror* enlisted Helen Worden to chronicle the Collyers one last time. She'd been freelancing since leaving the *World-Telegram* in 1944. The *Times* put Meyer Berger, the human-interest writer who started their "About New York" column, on the story. Arthur "Bugs" Baer, the *Journal-American* jester, visited the Collyer brownstone and reported, "These human packrats accumulated a stashaway of clusterings that out-shambled the ramifications of an idiot's inventory." Bugs liked to use big words, some of which were in the dictionary.

Worden was on the scene when the cops found Homer. Jacob Iglitzen, the druggist, had tipped her off at seven A.M. on March 21. She stood on the sidewalk in front of the house when a cop from Police Emergency Squad 6 pushed his head out of a second-floor window and waved at her.

"This is your baby, Miss Worden, and the final chapter's being written right now."

Newspaper copy editors compressed that final chapter into headlines like trash compactors in a junkyard:

ONE COLLYER DEAD, SECOND HUNTED

IN 5TH AVENUE PALACE OF JUNK

CROWD WAITS IN VAIN FOR GLIMPSE

OF STILL MISSING LANGLEY COLLYER

POLICE SMASH INTO COLLYER HOME;
MISSING HERMIT NOT ON TOP FLOOR

THOUSANDS GAPE AT COLLYER HOUSE

FIND COLLYER, WIN $1,500

2D COLLYER ELUDES 2D DAY OF HUNT,
POLICE FAIL TO FIND A SECRET TUNNEL

COLLYER HUNT REACHES
STRATEGIC SECOND FLOOR

COPS COMBING COLLYER "JUNKPILE"
WARNED OF DANGER OF A CAVE-IN

STILL SIFT MANSION JUNK
IN SEARCH FOR HERMIT

POLICE FAIL TO FIND
COLLYER IN HOUSE

COPS CONFUSED OVER
COLLYER JUNK DISPOSAL

COLLYER MANSION

YIELDS JUNK, CATS

FBI AIDS IN SEARCH

FOR MISSING COLLYER

TODAY'S COLLYER FINDINGS:

4 VIOLINS, A CORNET, TROMBONE AND CELLO

TIP ON MISSING COLLYER

SPURS FUTILE SEARCH

POLICE IN VAIN HUNT

FOR LANGLEY COLLYER

OLD-SIZE BILLS TIP

POLICE TO COLLYER CACHE

LANGLEY COLLYER REPORTED

GOING TO ATLANTIC CITY

COLLYER HOUSE YIELDS

26 MORE TONS OF DEBRIS

LANGLEY COLLYER FACES

ARREST ON GUN CHARGE

HOMER COLLYER

RITES TUESDAY;

PUBLIC BARRED

WATCH FOR LANGLEY

AT BROTHER'S RITES

HOMER COLLYER BURIED;

BROTHER IS STILL MISSING

COLLYER HOME SEARCH

"NIGHTMARE" TO POLICE

SKULLS FOUND IN COLLYER CRIB

BODY IN RIVER TURNS OUT

NOT TO BE LANGLEY COLLYER

BOOBY TRAPS GROW DEADLY

IN COLLYER INNER SANCTUM

JUNK TONNAGE PASSES 100

AT COLLYER HOUSE

DID LANGLEY END LIFE?

FRIEND RECALLS THREAT

Chapter 12
Requiem for a Featherweight

For fifteen years Uncle Harry staked out a small corner of Uncle Arthur's apartment. But in 1998, while shadow-boxing in the kitchen, he slipped on a shifting pile of papers and had to be hospitalized. From then on, Uncle Harry's sparring was confined to a Brooklyn nursing home. He died a year later, at eighty-six, penniless and clutterless.

Uncle Arthur wrote an obituary and spent Uncle Harry's legacy of two hundred dollars to have it printed in *The New York Times*. Harry wanted his opponents, his stablemates, and his fan club to know he had died a champion.

LIDZ – Harry H., April 5, 1999, age 86. Veteran of Abraham Lincoln International Brigade 1937. He will be missed by his brother, Arthur . . .

"If Harry had a hobby, like me, he might have lived longer," Uncle Arthur said with a sigh at his brother's graveside. "Trouble is, he smoked too much."

He came home from the cemetery with a handful of pebbles and scrapings of moss. "If I didn't collect, I'd be in a nuthouse by now," Uncle Arthur said. "It takes away the stress. It gives me patience, which is what a person needs."

But gathering *moss*?

"Patience." No rolling stone, he.

"Harry's gone," Uncle Arthur had told me after the accident. "The social worker says he can't come back until I clean up the apartment."

I asked: "So what's your plan?"

"I'm gonna buy a bus pass and visit Harry once a week."

Which just goes to show: Junk is thicker than blood.

Chapter 13

O Brother, Where Art Thou?

A Wall Street lawyer reported a sighting of Langley even before police began looking for him. The police search didn't begin until Monday morning, two days after Homer was found. The cops boarded up the house at five P.M. on Friday and essentially went home for the weekend.

Albert Stickney, the lawyer, was sure he'd seen Langley on Friday at Bleecker Street on the IRT Lexington Avenue local. A shabby but courtly old man caught his attention. After he saw photos in the *Post*, he thought he had seen the missing recluse. Stickney's Langley spotting was the first of many, very many.

McMullen made the formal identification of Homer's body at the Bellevue Hospital morgue, then rushed uptown to the West 123rd Street police station to get permission from relatives to forage through the junk.

"A man might be dying," he said.

Detectives argued that Langley might be out on one of his

twenty-four-hour shopping sprees. He walked as far as Williamsburg in Brooklyn for whole-wheat bread, they said. If he didn't show up by one P.M. on Monday, they'd send out a missing person's alarm and search the house.

The curious people parading by the house on Sunday afternoon were not so sanguine.

"He's right up there looking out the window, laughing at you," said one.

Scores of cars cruised by slowly, full of families out for a Sunday drive from as far away as Connecticut and New Jersey.

The only sign of life at the dark, malodorous house was a black cat that padded out from a hole in the damaged mahogany door and crossed the street.

On Monday, a crowd of two thousand clogged Fifth Avenue from sidewalk to rooftop. Police closed off two blocks. Newspaper reporters and photographers, television and newsreel cameramen pressed close as policemen and an emergency squad climbed a ladder to the roof. Radio newsmen broadcast play-by-play like announcers at a Yankees game.

"If Langley's in there he'll never come out with all these people here," McMullen said. "He probably has looked out, seen the crowd, and become frightened."

The searchers chopped through a skylight and found themselves confronted with a morass of Langley's salvage. Police and building inspectors hacked on through, tossing junk out through the hole to the roof, then to the backyard three stories below.

Two dressmaker dummies fell into the yard, then a couple of bicycles, crumbling tires and leather bike seats, a dozen gas chandeliers, a doll carriage, sheets in Braille from Homer's failed attempts to learn the system, yellowed photographs of 1890s bathing girls, including one the *Sun* reporter found "a particularly voluptuous blond with a saucy smile," an ad for cognac at two dollars a gallon from Flegenheimer Brothers in the Bronx, a certificate of merit for punctuality and good conduct awarded to Langley at Public School 69 for the week ending April 19, 1895, and a program for the February 27, 1914, production of *The Magic Flute* at the Metropolitan Opera. Perhaps Langley had taken his mother.

"Gosh," said William B. Collyer, a cousin from Yonkers. "What a bunch of junk!"

The *Sun* reported that the police "worked in relays, saying that the stench in the building made it impossible to endure more than ten or fifteen minutes.

"The men in blue invariably came out men in white, uniforms thick with cobwebs and dust which covered everything in the building inches thick."

Even as the police were burrowing into the house, a Langley doppelgänger was reported looking for a room by three different Brooklynites.

Anthony Soranno, a real estate broker in Brooklyn Heights, told police the elderly man came in and said, "I've lived in a place for many years and now I have to get out."

A soft rain fell intermittently as the police worked and the day grew dark early. Searchlights powered by a portable generator outlined them like figures in film noir.

They finally boarded up the windows and piled up the junk beyond the high fence at the 128th Street side of house.

"We will be back tomorrow and go over this place inch by inch," said Inspector Joseph Goldstein, of the Tenth Division.

Diehard remnants of the crowd passed by for one final look, kicking aside hundreds of yellow half-price tickets for *Angela*, a musical comedy that played at the Century Theater in 1929.

The next day opened with Langley reported once again in the subway. This time on an F train at the Church Avenue Station in Brooklyn. Police stopped seven F trains, but found no Langley.

Jake Iglitzen, the druggist, announced that he had received a letter purportedly from Langley demanding the hunt be called off.

"He's too smart for them, an educated man, a learned man. He will be back. When they go for good, he will be back. In the night."

Was Langley on the run?

William Harris, a neighbor from across 128th Street, thought he might be.

"Maybe he's dead," Harris told reporters. "Maybe he's so far away he's never coming back to New York. Maybe he had bundles of money there. Maybe, as soon as Homer died, he got the first train way out."

Henry Matourney, a furtive little man, beckoned to reporters standing vigil outside the house.

"You'll find that man in the subway," he said, confidentially. "Man likes the dark. He lived that way all his life, like caves. You look through subways, you find that man."

But Miriam Fasin, from 132nd Street, disagreed.

"I used to give him sugar because he had no ration book. We used to visit each other. I would sit on his steps and talk to him."

She was a small black woman in a plain coat with a kerchief tied around her head. She remembered she had last chatted with Langley on a warm day in late February.

" 'How are you, Mr. Langley?' " I asked.

" 'Not so good,' he said. 'My brother isn't well. If he dies I'm going to jump in the river. He's all I have to live for. Besides, the police would hold me because I didn't have a doctor for him. I'd rather be dead than go through all that. When Homer dies tell them to look for me in the river.' "

Hyman Schwartz, who ran a butcher shop on East 121st Street at Third Avenue, told the *Sun* perhaps the most bizarre tale. He had been giving the Collyer brothers meat every Saturday night for nearly thirty years, he said.

Homer came in first in 1918, the year his father moved out. He bought a pound of frankfurters.

"The next Saturday night he came back," Schwartz recalled. "He waited till all my customers were gone and then he said he didn't have any money and could he have a pound of meat."

Schwartz gave him the meat. Homer came back every Saturday night for the next fifteen years until he showed up one Saturday with Langley.

"He said his eyes had been hurting him and he couldn't see anymore," Schwartz said. "Langley led him out of the shop.

"I never saw him again. The next Saturday Langley showed up. He said Homer was blind. I gave him the meat. From then on he came every Saturday night until February 22. After that he didn't come anymore."

Schwartz and his strange customer seemed to get along pretty well.

"I could listen to him for hours," the butcher said. "But his English was so high I couldn't understand half of what he said."

Langley had said that newspaper stories about his wealth were lies. He told Schwartz he was broke.

"He used to scrape garbage out of the cans along the street," Schwartz said. "I asked him why. 'People throw away lots that is good,' he said. 'I cut out the rotten part and eat the rest.'"

After once seeing Langley pick over garbage cans in 1941, a Lenox Avenue baker started giving him day-old rolls twice a week until he disappeared. But Langley had to strip old-style dollar bills from a scrapbook to pay for the wine he bought three times a month from a Lexington Avenue liquor store.

Two dozen police and New York City Housing Department workers continued to sift patiently through the corridors of junk on the third floor, separating possible "valuables" from outright trash they tossed out. The first Department of Sanitation truck carried away 6,424 pounds, the second slightly less. The department ordered its workers sprayed with DDT before they entered the brownstone.

Building engineers pulled a crew out of the basement and made them work from the top down. The inspectors feared the house might collapse like a house of cards if junk was pulled out of the lower floors. They thought it might be holding the place up.

Workmen on the third floor found pistols, shotguns, rifles, bullets, and shotgun shells, which some thought made Langley liable to gun-law violations. A cavalry saber and a French bayonet were probably not illegal. A high wind blew letters into the street, where folks in the crowd plucked them out of the air for souvenirs. A brisk sidewalk sale began, with the market price set at a dollar a letter. By the end of the week, the price was five dollars.

Perhaps the most poignant find was the half dozen tickets to the annual excursion of the Trinity Church Sunday School on Saturday, July 8, 1905. The brothers were baptized at Trinity Church and they taught Sunday school classes there. The church offered to bury Homer.

Langley's deadly booby traps threatened investigators everywhere and every day. A patrolman named Raymond Stack, pushing into the main hall, triggered an avalanche of jugs, fluorescent tubes, lumber, baled papers, scraps of metal, and parts from an old radio that poured down on his head. He escaped battered but unhurt.

Detectives climbing through a narrow passage on the packed stairs to the second floor tripped deadfall that brought down two seventy-five-pound, two-foot-square chunks of concrete and a cascade of tin cans, crowbars, and "inutile material" – urine and excrement, the Collyer legacy preserved in jars.

"Yesterday's discoveries," the *Sun* concluded, "including bottled slops that rained down the stairway along with man-killing weights, clinched the brothers' claim – in case there was any doubt – to the title of worst housekeepers in New York, if not the world."

Police hoped Langley would show up at Homer's funeral on April Fools' Day.

Homer was buried in an oaken coffin with bronze handles, sealed by order of the Health Department, as if starvation were contagious. A simple wreath of daffodils, snapdragons, and lemon leaves tied with a lavender bow lay on the coffin during the service in the gray stone abbey of Cypress Hills Cemetery in Brooklyn. The Reverend Dr. Charles T. Bridgeman, a curate from Trinity Church, read the committal service from the Book of Common Prayer.

Fifty-three mourners attended the funeral, including seventeen cousins, one named Langley, from Cobleskill, New York.

The only neighbors from Harlem were Laura Sullivan and her five-year-old son, Courtney, who lived a block north of the brothers on Fifth Avenue.

"He was a good man, if a bit of an eccentric," Sullivan said in a bit of understatement.

Homer was interred in the family plot about a quarter mile from the abbey with his mother and father and grandmother. Three detectives and about thirty reporters and photographers hovered among the tombstones, hoping for an appearance by Langley.

He didn't show.

Chapter 14
The Junkman Cometh

Langley's photo was wired around the country. Fifteen hundred were handed out and posted in hospitals and train stations. The FBI stepped in and issued an eleven-state bulletin; sightings were immediately reported in practically every one.

Langleys popped up all over the East Coast, hitchhiking to Hendersonville, North Carolina; boarding a bus in Barnegat, New Jersey, for Atlantic City; trout fishing in the Adirondacks; and eating frozen custard in Newark.

A guard at the Federal Building in Manhattan was positive a ragged old man he had stopped was Langley. Andrei Gromyko, the Soviet ambassador to the United Nations, said to another delegate: "Who knows, we might find out today where Langley Collyer is." An elderly, scruffy-looking New Yorker with a Langley-like mustache, fed up with being bothered, hoisted a hand-lettered sign that read: I AM NOT LANGLEY COLLYER, PLEASE!

Brooklynites were still on red alert. A conductor on an IND train in Flatbush started a chain reaction when he was sure he had spotted Langley. He shouted to a stationmaster at Church Avenue, who flashed the Board of Transportation, who alerted their special police and city police. They converged on the Borough Hall–Jay Street station to meet the train. They held the doors open and stared hard at the passengers. None of them was Langley.

In the Bronx, a body floating in Pugsley's Creek was briefly believed to be Langley. The elderly drowned man had gray hair and a gray mustache. He turned out to be a gent formerly resident on a houseboat moored in the creek.

The happiest Langley lookalike was Joe Gould, the Greenwich Village bard immortalized by Joseph Mitchell in *The New Yorker* as "Professor Seagull." He was pleased to go along with two *Daily News* reporters who routed him out of bed, convinced that he was Langley.

"They tried to insult me with two bottles of ale," the professor said. "I swallowed the insult, then admitted I am not Langley Collyer."

The ballyhoo gas balloon had inflated so much by this time, even the *Daily News* was tired of the story.

"We find ourselves wishing the New York policemen would

just sweep Langley's place up a little more," an editorialist wrote, "and then quietly steal away, maybe leaving a little bowl of milk for him on the doorstep."

The police felt pretty much the same way. They had believed almost from the start that Langley was dead somewhere in the house. But after two weeks one hundred tons of junk had been removed and Langley was still missing.

At the end of March, the Herculean task of cleaning out the Collyer home was turned over to a six-man crew of professional movers at 120 dollars a day. They ripped out the basement entrance and emptied the law library. Rare treasures surfaced like amphorae in an archaeological dig.

Susie Collyer's unfinished knitting. Dr. Herman's forms for "Habit Forming Drugs." A two-headed baby floating in formaldehyde. Thirteen ornate mantel clocks, one in a metal bust of a girl whose ears and bodice dripped coins. Langley's sheet music for Chopin's Nocturnes. Two pipe organs. A clavichord. A trombone. A cornet. An accordion. Five violins, including a Georgus Rugeri Cremona, 1762; a George Paolo Magini Brescia, 1784; and a cello, wrapped in cloth and labeled "Stradivarius 1727." All fake.

Dr. Herman's electrical therapeutic apparatus known as a static machine turned up on the first floor. The ten-foot-tall, five-foot-wide metal-and-glass cabinet containing numerous balls and cranks, bell and whistles, had been used in the treatment of rheumatism and arthritis at the end of the nineteenth century.

A small cabinet that looked like a calliope was an early X-ray machine. Prowling through the parlors, Helen Worden opened the lid on another box and found a Davis and Kidder's "Magneto Electric Machine."

A canopied wooden crib contained two human skulls, a spine, hands, feet, and a rib cage, perhaps a disassembled medical specimen left behind when the doctor departed.

Herman's gladstone was found with all his instruments intact and, sadly, a brand-new shirt, size 15, with a bright scarlet tie, left unworn in a box never opened for twenty-nine years. A birthday card dated October 3, 1918, read, "To Langley, with many happy returns this day, Pop." The doctor left the Macy's price tag attached. The shirt cost ninety-seven cents.

As the workmen shoveled more and more stuff out, the Collyer house became a stop on the New York tourist circuit. "Rubberneck buses" passed by two or three times a day.

On Good Friday, a messenger from the Ballerina Flower Shop on Madison Avenue left a potted lily on the stoop. The pot was wrapped in green tissue paper and tied with a yellow ribbon. The card – "For Langley" – was unsigned. And he never picked it up.

Easter came and went. Homer had been dead sixteen days.

On a cold night two days later, H. Walter Skidmore, the public administrator in charge of Collyer affairs, and his assistant, Archie Matthews, scrambled through the hills of debris.

"Hey, Archie, I've got that odor again," he cried. "Look under that bump of papers."

Matthews reached into the pile.

"Jesus Christ, I've got him by the toe."

Chapter 15

If He Hollers, Let Him Go

Langley Collyer was found.

He had been pinned to the floor by one of his own booby traps. He lay no more than ten feet from where Homer had been found. His body was wedged between a mahogany chest and the frame of an old sewing machine. Detectives said he was turned toward his brother, his arm and gnarled fingers stretched out as if in supplication.

Langley smothered under the debris that had fallen on him, said Dr. Thomas A. Gonzales, the chief medical examiner. Langley had been dead at least a month. He had died before Homer.

Lieutenant Charles Meyer of the Missing Persons Bureau sketched a final portrait of Langley.

"No cap, baldish, hair seven inches long, moustache wispy, three days growth of beard. The rats had eaten half the face, both hands, both feet and part of the right thigh, but he was still identifiable."

Langley was dressed as strangely in death as in life. He wore four pairs of pants, but no underwear, a herringbone jacket, a red flannel bathrobe, a gray dungaree jacket, and a rat-eaten morning coat. Knotted at his neck as an ascot was an onion sack. A burlap bag was fastened to his shoulder.

Police took more than two hours to push aside enough debris to move Langley's body and carry it out of the building.

Laborers returned the next morning and took sixteen tons of trash from the room in which the brothers were found dead. So far 136 tons had been removed from the building.

Langley was buried next to Homer in the family plot at Cypress Hills.

"There goes a misunderstood man," McMullen said in his graveside eulogy. "He devoted days and nights to taking care of blind and crippled Homer.

"Langley was one of the most exemplary characters I've known in life or in literature," he sobbed as the coffin was lowered into the grave. "He was good and he was kind."

And he got two more wreaths than Homer.

About fifty people filled the abbey, including most of the cousins who had shown up for Homer's send-off. About one hundred more mourners stood outside.

"As you know," McMullen said as he left the cemetery, "Langley and Homer hated publicity. They would have gotten a kick out of seeing only two reporters and two photographers here today."

Chapter 16
Fool For Love

When Uncle Harry went to the nursing home, the pretense to order that he had imposed on the apartment went with him. Uncle Arthur quickly expanded his collections into his brother's meager space. Now nearly every cubic inch of the apartment was full and virtually every surface was covered with heaps of stuff that mounted toward the ceiling. Uncle Arthur hated a vacuum.

Tangled mounds of twine and electrical cord climbed up gentle slopes of newspapers still in their plastic sleeves. A riot of shirts and jackets slopped out of stained brown grocery bags and onto the grubby carpet. The stove and the kitchen counters disappeared from view, lost under a couple of feet of cans, bottles, and Calder-like mobiles that Uncle Arthur had fashioned out of clothespins and coat hangers. He packed the bedroom closet with tabloids from the Carter administration. "I haven't opened the door since 1978," he said.

Thick layers of grunge coated the bathroom walls. The shower curtain and the soap were black. And if you turned the knobs on the faucet, roaches literally sprayed out.

What had been charming and actually comforting to me as a child now had become downright appalling. I would no more want a fanatical hoarder like Uncle Arthur living next door than Hannibal Lecter.

I found myself echoing my father. I demanded that Uncle Arthur clean up his act: "It's a fire hazard. It's a health hazard. It's not junk, it's garbage." Uncle Arthur parried me as he did my dad: "Yeah, but it's mine."

I imagined staging my own commando raid on his bunker. I'd come armed with brooms, mops, and disinfectants. I'd leave Uncle Arthur's place tidy, spotless, and sanitary – and Uncle Arthur heartbroken. Uncle Arthur was, after all, defined by his junk. He loved it. He needed it. So I kept putting off my mop-up operation.

His Philadelphia relatives were less tolerant and more impatient. They tried to shanghai Uncle Arthur into an old-age home in the suburbs that would allow him his incontinent cat but not his junk. Uncle Arthur took one look at this neat, clean, well-lighted place and said, "I won't go. Everybody's old."

He was only eighty-five.

Uncle Arthur's social worker told me: "Don't let them send him. I've seen well-meaning relatives do this over and over. Your uncle wouldn't live six months."

Before I realized it, a lawyer was hired, documents were signed, and a twenty-thousand-dollar deposit was demanded. Uncle Arthur balked. He didn't know he'd have to give up his apartment. And he didn't want to. He short-circuited the deal when he said he'd pay only half. No one offered the other half. I stepped in, threatening to bring in my own lawyer. Uncle Arthur stayed put.

I had always figured Uncle Arthur would die like a Collyer, surrounded by the artifacts of his life and the decades of newspapers he had saved to read in his old age, not smothered by cleanliness in a sterile retirement home. I never imagined that at eighty-five he'd get caught up in a web of lust and betrayal.

Early in the spring of 2000, I got a call from Yuli Gollarza, the super's wife. A bubbly, buxom Venezuelan, she had taken a liking to Uncle Arthur. She worried about him living alone with his hoard. She bought him food, fixed his meals, cut his hair. But she didn't want to confront his junk.

Yuli told me she had found Uncle Arthur in the lobby of his

building. He was paler than usual and he sat quite passively on a red vinyl couch, his face buried in his hands.

"What's wrong, Uncle Arthur?" Yuli asked. Even she called him "Uncle."

He wept openly.

Yuli put her arm around his shoulders and asked as gently as she could: "Uncle Arthur, won't you tell me what's wrong?"

He heaved a very big sigh and took a big breath.

"She took all my money and never came back."

Uncle Arthur confessed he'd met a young Russian woman. On Valentine's Day, she had sat next to him on a bus bound for Brighton Beach and had chatted him up. "My name is Ann Ross," she had said, improbably. "What's yours?" He was smitten, once again. She suggested lunch. He said okay. He, of course, declined to pay. She persisted. He paid. They met again, and again. Uncle Arthur had a secret love.

Ann visited his apartment. She proposed sex.

"I'm eighty-five," Uncle Arthur told her. "Nothing works!"

What happened next? As Boris Karloff once said, some things it is better not to know.

She had a sick aunt, Ann said. She asked to borrow one hundred dollars. Uncle Arthur hadn't lent anybody a nickel since roughly 1927. She charmed him. He gave her a hundred dollars. She repaid him.

Her aunt got sicker. She borrowed five hundred dollars, then five thousand dollars. She paid him back each time. Then her aunt needed seventy-five thousand dollars for an operation. Uncle Arthur withdrew most of his life savings from four different banks and gave her a certified check.

Ann went missing. Uncle Arthur called her cell-phone number a dozen times a day. The line she once answered just rang and rang and rang. But he still called her "my girlfriend."

"I really fell for her," said Uncle Arthur. "She was really pretty. She promised she'd pay me back."

The police said there was nothing they could do. He was the victim of a perfect crime. "It's like she welched on a debt," a detective explained. "Unfortunately, it's not illegal not to repay someone."

The cops asked Uncle Arthur to describe his girlfriend. He reached into his pocket and withdrew a folded piece of newspaper. It was a Victoria's Secret ad featuring a busty model in lingerie. "She looks sorta like this," he said.

Ross's bunco artistry reinforced Uncle Arthur's distrust of women.

"Women are too smart," he said. "That's why I've never

been married. They want this and that. My brother Danny used to say you can't trust 'em. He was right."

Uncle Arthur recalled precisely that his only previous sexual encounter occurred on May 11, 1938, when he was twenty-three.

"It was a call girl, a colored woman," he said. "She took me to an apartment in Harlem. Not hers, just some apartment at 2080 Fifth Avenue. And it happened. It wasn't fun. It just didn't come out, and I never did it again."

In an odd coincidence, 2080 Fifth is right next door to the Collyer brownstone. Helen Worden broke the Collyer story exactly three months later. Fannie and her two most devoted sons still lived only three blocks away. She moved them out to the Bronx about two weeks later.

After his fling with Ann, Uncle Arthur really felt vulnerable. People might think he couldn't take care of himself. His Philadelphia relatives might commit him.

"I sort of suspect I might get evicted," he confided. "My landlord says my junk is too heavy for the ceiling below me, and people in my building are complaining about the mice. A third of them are against me."

"Let me clean out the apartment," I said.

"Yeah," he said reluctantly. "Maybe it's time to give it up."

I shipped him off to the Jersey shore. Then five friends and I began to deconstruct his collage of junk.

Uncle Arthur's single fifteen-watt chandelier bulb lit our work. In seven hours, we never got out of the living room. It took five hours just to get to the floor. We filled 417 extra-large heavy-duty contractor bags and hauled them down on the elevator eight to ten at a time. Not to mention dozens of rickety chairs, dressers, cabinets, shopping carts, and Uncle Harry's folding cot. We filled the Dumpster and lined bags up against the wall until the super begged us to stop. The trash collectors took a month to carry it all away.

The super and his crew took over and spent the next nine days cleaning, repairing, painting, and fumigating. Yuli put a new blanket on Uncle Arthur's bed, a new curtain on the shower, a mat in the bathroom, and shaggy covers on the toilet tank and seat. She threw him a party and decorated the shiny new apartment with Chinese lanterns and balloons and baked him a cake. Everybody in The Argyle came to welcome him back.

"Even the third who are against me," Uncle Arthur said.

He had a good time but he still was dubious about all the space around him.

"For one thing, the traffic noise is very loud now," he said in a little soliloquy. "The junk blocked the sounds out so I didn't hear them. I'm getting used to having space, but it's still empty space.

"To tell the truth, I'm a little bit disappointed. I thought more stuff would be saved. I have sort of an empty feeling, like I've been robbed or something.

"It's a little hard to see the stuff leave. I've lost memories of my four brothers and my mother. But things happen, what can you do? I'm too old to worry anymore. I just want quiet and peace now. I don't even put on the television. Well, once in a long while I do.

"The emptiness is a little hard to get used to. It makes me feel hollow. My junk was like a friend, another person, another cat. Sort of a freedom, it was. I'd saved it in my own way. I put so much work into saving – years and years, and it's suddenly gone. It's like somebody had died, a fire or an earthquake."

I stood in Uncle Arthur's refurbished bachelor pad, listening to him pine for the clutter of the first eighty-five years of his youth. I dropped a piece of the Entenmann's coffee cake I'd brought. Uncle Arthur shuffled over to a closet and pulled out a broom. He swept up the crumbs. My god, I thought, he has reformed.

But when I visited him a few months later, I found his desk

again covered with circulars, handbills, and a few traffic tickets, and the floor carpeted with newspapers. "To soak up Wagging's pee," he said. I had a strong suspicion – stronger even than the smell of cat piss – why they were piling up. I peeked in his bedroom closet and saw a small cache of sugar packets. "I used to have them from a hundred countries," he said. "I'm starting over."

Chapter 17
Laugh Boys Laugh

I was foraging through a closet near the end of the cleanup when I finally found a small gem, the composition book with Uncle Leo's poems. It was bound in Saran Wrap and wedged behind 134 unopened jars of Chock full o'Nuts coffee – Uncle Arthur's hedge against a Colombian embargo.

They were the poems Uncle Leo wrote until he went mad in the Harlem tenement. He was a strange, sad, lonely guy, a ghosty man suspended in a private dream. He was isolated from his mother and four brothers, and mocked and laughed at by almost everyone else in his life.

I unwrapped the schoolbook and saw a handwriting exactly like my father's, a slightly antiquated script with lots of flourishes. Uncle Leo's poems were alternately bitter, romantic, or prosaic.

I hear you rant and raise your pious mugs
And look at me as though I were what you are
You prostituted hirelings of a diseased civilization
You lowdown morons, worse than stinking privies
Call me a fool, raving and inconsistent
Call me what you damn please
At least you know what I think of you
And your cankerous leprous methods.

He wrote "Like a Ghost" to a mysterious Miss S.B. on October 10, 1934.

Like a ghost I walk the streets
Trying to regain my love
Like a ghost I walk the streets
But she gives me the air . . . like a ghost

And he wrote "Fooled" to Miss S.B. on the same very productive day.

Fooled fooled again by my pregnant imagination
Such is the stuff that poets are made of

"The 3rd Degree" is perhaps indefinable.

I'm ready for my degree
All I need is a gallows and some rope

Uncle Leo walked down to the river at dusk and sat alone with his thoughts. He wrote the prose poem "Hudson River Blues" as night fell on October 2, 1932.

Electric lights, gaiety, sadness, the river, the bridge in its splendor, the trees gently blown. Here and there everywhere, quiet and noisy, changing forever. Words said before – lost no one knows, ferryboats gliding, smooth now the river, soon rough the waters, changing forever. And in my heart, sadness enduring, stillness required to collect my distraught nerves. Yet the surge of life onward impels me to listen, to the clang and the clamor, the streams of the active. The heart of the city, the lifeblood, the throbbing, the pulse beating turmoil, creation is calling. The dead they are nothing, the living are something, yet here I am outside of life and its meaning, perhaps I'm mistaken – for yet I am breathing – though song of the saddest – though song of the wretched – condemned and despised – yes despised.

He had gone on the road in the summer of 1932 like hundreds of thousands of other young men of his Depression generation. He swung out of New York on an arc through Pennsylvania and Ohio and on down the rivers to New Orleans. And he wrote verse in the style of Whitman, the Sampler, not the poet.

In myriad places have I strode
And I have seen the purple southern skies
Yes I have dwelt beneath the city ken
And rambled hither thither and away

But he returned to Fannie and the boys after a couple of months. He had given up the freedom of the vast America of Walt Whitman for the cramped tenement apartment of the Lidzes. His next trip was to the madhouse. The final poem in the book, the ambiguously titled "A Happy Thought?," foretold the fate of those two other Harlem ghosty men.

Laugh boys laugh
A few years more and we'll all be dead
And new faces will come and cackle in this place
Laugh boys laugh
For a heavy doom is awaiting you

Chapter 18
Yard Sale of the Century

The first sale of the "Collyer Collection" was more slapstick than Sotheby's.

The choice stuff from the mansion went on sale at a city warehouse in downtown Manhattan two months after Langley was found dead.

"What do you want it for?" yelled Sidney Salomon, the sharp-tongued city marshal who ran the auction. "You must be out of your head paying so much for this junk."

Salomon was annoyed that there were more gawkers than bidders among the three hundred people squeezed into a seventh-floor loft of the old Journal-American Building. At ten A.M., he started selling 150 items culled from the 136 tons carted out of the mansion in Harlem. The sightseers made it hard to hear "serious bidders."

Max Schaefer, the proprietor of Hubert's Museum and Flea Circus, was very serious.

"It's hard to get customers inside in the summer," Schaefer told reporters. "A few of these items ought to turn the trick."

He spent three hundred dollars on a crib, a school desk in which Homer had penned his initials, two cornets, a bugle, and two rusty bayonets. Perhaps not crowd pleasers in themselves, but they had great provenance. Schaefer was disappointed that the two-headed baby wasn't in the sale.

Nelson Gidding, a writer from the Upper East Side, bought six big floppy-brimmed Panama hats for twenty-two dollars.

"I jumped right up and came down," he said. "Panama hats of this sort are hard to get these days."

He said he'd wear them in Haiti, where he frequently hunted for buried treasure.

Jacob Lubetkin, of Ye Olde Curiosity Shoppe in Greenwich Village, and a lawyer named Braunstein bid spiritedly at ten dollars a clip on an eight-foot mahogany grandfather clock that played "The Campbells Are Coming."

"We're now selling the biggest piece of junk in the house," the auctioneer cried. "Don't duck out on it."

Lubetkin won at $310, the highest price of the day. He planned to put it in the window of his shoppe.

"It'll make a striking advertisement," he said.

Over the next couple of hours Salomon and his aides sold off two generations of the Collyer family heritage at dime-store prices:

Susie Collyer's hope chests, brimming with silk, wool, damask, brocade, and fine monogrammed linens, none ever used. Violet and Jockey Club perfume mingled with dressing-table bric-a-brac.

The boys' toy trains, still shiny and new, in sawdust-filled boxes. A battered bicycle perhaps crashed by Langley or Homer.

Family portraits in heavy velvet-lined frames.

Phonograph records from early in the twentieth century: "When Father Laid the Carpet on the Stairs," "Nobody in Town Can Bake a Sweet Jelly Roll Like Mine" and "Can't Get Lovin' Blues."

At noon the sale was over and the Collyer Collection had sold for $1,892.50.

Ten days later Salomon went uptown to the sagging brownstone to unload the thirty tons of junk that was left. The *Times* reported he was not a man given to the suave approach. He slapped a dusty piano, wiped his hands, and demanded: "Who'll give a buck for this broken-down relic?"

No one bid.

"On to bigger and better junk."

He offered four bookcases.

"No books, but solid mahogany. A buck starts it off."

No bid.

"Another piano," Salomon said. "It's in excellent condition."

"Thirty-five dollars."

He could not believe his ears, according to the *Times*.

"What?"

"Fofty-five dollars."

"Sold," the auctioneer thundered.

The dust was heavy and the room fetid. The visitors breathed through their hankies.

"I'll sell everything in the joint right now," Salomon boomed.

Carlos Martin, a Third Avenue secondhand dealer, bid one hundred dollars and got the lot. He hauled away seven truckloads of "claptrap." And he managed to sell most of the stuff within a couple of weeks.

Langley's newspapers brought Martin a dime apiece. He lamented that he had only saved a couple of hundred of the thousands in the house.

"If I had taken them all," he said, "I would have been a rich man."

He made money off glassware, cameras, chandeliers, and a stash of 1913 automobile license plates. But his biggest sale was four pianos and an organ that went for fifteen dollars. Disappointing were the thousands of cans stacked neatly in the house. Martin thought he had a complete grocery. Unfortunately they were empty.

He had his sentimental side. He didn't try to sell Langley's 1910 blue-and-white bathing suit. "I've held on to it somehow," he said. "I keep it in a back room where it won't be likely to sell."

The proceeds of both auctions went into the pool "heirs" would claim. They hoped for a jackpot. Old Doc Collyer, after all, was supposed to have owned half the New York waterfront.

Fifty-six "Collyers," cousins and second cousins and one lady from Pittsburgh who claimed to be a sister of Langley and Homer, showed up to claim their chunk of the estate. Most of them had never even seen the brothers, let alone visited them in Harlem. The only sister they had had died in 1880 at the age of four months and was buried with Susie and Herman in Cypress Hills Cemetery.

Genealogical charts more than five feet long were compiled to trace relationships among the claimants. A Surrogate Court judge decided that twenty-three could share the estate that turned out to be just fifty-one thousand dollars after debts and back taxes were paid.

The ramshackle house at 2078 Fifth Avenue was condemned as unsafe and torn down less than six months after the brothers died. The *Times* reported that the junk-filled house was now a junk-filled lot covered with scraggly weeds and rusting beer cans.

Passersby ignored it.

Chapter 19
If You Knew Susie

People began explaining the Collyers before they were even in their graves. Everyone wanted to rationalize the irrational. Most blamed Mom.

Helen Worden started it off: "Perhaps the mother might have been the answer since she was the most dominant character in the family.

"It was the mother who made all the decisions. They lived for her, she for them. The tragedy was that by her overpowering devotion she rendered helpless the two human beings she loved best. After her death, they were utterly without initiative."

The *Post* consulted Dr. Leopold Beliak, "the world famous psychiatrist," who declared the brothers sane.

Dr. Beliak suggested that enormous anxiety had caused the two educated, brilliant men to withdraw from society.

"They identified with their mother," he said. "Their Victorian clothing means identification with the period when their mother was a girl. Perhaps their fear of their father grew to include all mankind."

The Freudian theory reached its zenith in Leon Edel's speculations in *PM*. Psychiatrists, he said, describe Langley as "a classic textbook case of infantile regression. His life was a journey back to the security of the womb instead of the normal adult journey away from it. The principal factor was an attachment, intense and deep, to his mother." The French have a lovely phrase for it – *nostalgie de la boue*, literally, homesickness for the primal ooze of embryohood.

There was widespread agreement that the Collyers' minds had been as disordered as their home.

The *Journal-American* found psychiatrists who explained that, like children, the two grown men could not discriminate between articles of real value and those that they thought important.

"They apparently put equal value on everything that interested them – pianos, balls of string, gilt-edged securities."

Uncle Arthur felt the same way. Used shoelaces are as important to him as Fabergé eggs were to Malcolm Forbes.

"Maybe it's something I missed in my childhood," he says.

"Like something big. The thing is you don't have to pay for junk. It's free."

But in the radical left-wing *New Masses*, the novelist Howard Fast offered the Marxist dialectic:

"Who killed Langley Collyer?

"Property killed him.

"Property fell on him and squashed him like a bug."

Dorothy Day took an uncompromising Christian Socialist view in the *Catholic Worker*:

"This story seems to me a vision of hell," she wrote in May 1947, "a very literal and appalling sample of the hell that awaits the acquisitive, the greedy, the accumulators, the seekers after markets, wealth, power, prestige, exclusiveness, empire, dominion, of everything opposed to the common good. Here were two old men who epitomized to the nth degree suspicion and hatred of their fellows and a desire to gather together to themselves, everything they could lay their hands on."

Today we might call them obsessive-complusive and pack them off to the contemporary equivalent of Dr. Beliak, who might prescribe Xanax.

Walter Skidmore, the public administrator, told Helen Worden he found the answer in an old letter Langley wrote but never sent.

The envelope was addressed to a girl. Langley, Worden said, in the most formal English, described his anguish when the young woman abruptly stopped her music lessons.

He went to her home. Her mother told him the girl had gone away. For a long time he paced back and forth on the street where she lived. He sometimes sat on the stoop of a house opposite until dawn. But he never saw her again.

"Love does queer things to you," Skidmore said. "If you ask me, it left Langley a little touched."

Langley and Uncle Arthur were both a little touched, maybe downright crazy. They collected without discrimination. They valued shoelaces and tin cans as much as Old Masters and grand pianos. They tried to build personal utopias behind drawn shades and locked shutters from oddments of their childhood, mementos of their families, and parapets of newspapers. And, inevitably perhaps, they found themselves trapped by their own fantasies.

Chapter 20

Subterranean Homesick Blues

Nothing remains of the ghosty house in Harlem. The city has put a pocket park on the northwest corner of 128th Street and Fifth Avenue. It's pleasant in early spring with daffodils blooming and grass freshly green behind an iron fence. In place of the towering elm, a dozen sycamores shade three benches, backed up against a peeling Black Nationalist mural on the wall of the house next door. A Parks Department sign warns: NO ALCOHOL, GAMBLING OR ILLEGAL SUBSTANCES. The gate is securely locked.

On the west side of Fifth Avenue, three brownstones remain from the Collyer era, in various states of repair or disrepair. A bit of gentrification is in progress on the corner and along 128th Street; 2080 Fifth, where Uncle Arthur tried to lose his virginity, is handsomely restored and protected with lots of window bars and American flags.

Still surviving across Fifth Avenue are most of the brownstones from which people watched Homer's body come out of 2078 in the police body bag. The corner building is gone and a weekend bazaar offers "antiques and preowned furniture," which the Collyers could have stocked infinitely.

Mount Morris Park at 124th Street, where Langley filled his demijohns of water on his postmidnight rounds, is now Marcus Garvey Park and the ghosts are all African-American.

In Cypress Hills Cemetery, the Collyer gravesite is just down the hill from where Mae West resides in a locked abbey. The entrance to the cemetery is on Jamaica Avenue in Brooklyn where the BMT line turns south onto Crescent Avenue. Uncle Leo passed there every day on the way to his job as a paperhanger. He mentions it in "The Paperhanger's Lament."

Homer and Langley lie side by side in a grassy gravesite, just below Archimedes Way, not far from Thanatopolis Drive, together in death as in life. Jackie Robinson is not very far away. He joined the Brooklyn Dodgers the year the Collyers were buried.

"We have the real people of Brooklyn," says William Moloney, office manager at the cemetery. "The originals. We're full of the street names of Brooklyn – Van Wyck, Clinton, Fulton."

Piet Mondrian, the neoplasticist abstract artist who painted

Broadway Boogie Woogie, ended up here, as did Kate and Maggie Fox, the Rochester spiritualists defrocked by Houdini, and P. T. Barnum, who might have booked the Collyers as a sideshow act.

Mae West's mom lived just a block away. Mae visited every week when she was in Gotham. Neighbors said she was just folks. Nobody comes up to see her anytime these days. She left strict orders forbidding visitors to her tomb. She was even laid out on a marble shelf in the dead of night like Susie Collyer.

Gentleman Jim Corbett's in the abbey, too. And so is Paderewski, the pianist whose notices drove Langley from the concert stage.

The brothers share their plot with their mother and father and numerous other Collyers. But in this old Victorian cemetery full of marble obelisks, broken columns, and draped urns, not a single stone marks the Collyer graves. Homer and Langley have recovered in death the anonymity they sought in life.

Acknowledgments

This book could not have been written without the help of my collaborator, Carl Schoettler, who played Homer to my Langley. Or was it the other way around? Through the years, Carl's stubborn integrity and impeccable standards have challenged and inspired me. On the subject of his influence, he once said, "About the only thing more forgettable than yesterday's newspaper is yesterday's newspaperman. The big difference is that you can't wrap fish in an old newspaperman."

Thanks to Kathie Borowitz, Rob Buchanan, Kris Dahl, Karen Rinaldi, Joel Rose, Paul Somerson, and the Argyle cleanup crew: Lex Braes, Leon Gollarza, Dana Kennedy, Mark Moskowitz, and Tomas Muscionico.

Cover photo of Uncle Arthur amid his junk by Gigi Cohen.

Franz Lidz is the author of the memoir *Unstrung Heroes: My Improbable Life with Four Impossible Uncles*. Born in Manhattan, he lives on a six-acre farm just north of the Mason-Dixon Line with two llamas (Edgar and Ogar), two dogs (Huck and Ella), three cats (Yojimbo, Sanjuro, and Mr. H), nine chickens (don't ask), two daughters (Gogo and Daisy Daisy), and one wife (Maggie).

A NOTE ON THE TYPE

The text of this book is set in Linotype Sabon, named after the type founder, Jacques Sabon. It was designed by Jan Tschichold and jointly developed by Linotype, Monotype, and Stempel, in response to a need for a typeface to be available in identical form for mechanical hot metal composition and hand composition using foundry type.

Tschichold based his design for Sabon roman on a font engraved by Garamond, and Sabon italic on a font by Granjon. It was first used in 1966 and has proved an enduring modern classic.